Euripides' Bacchae

Euripides' Bacchae

Translation, Introduction and Notes
Stephen J. Esposito
Boston University

Focus Classical Library
Focus Publishing/R Pullins Company
Newburyport MA 01950

THE FOCUS CLASSICAL LIBRARY
Series Editors • James Clauss and Stephen Esposito

Aristophanes: Acharnians • Jeffrey Henderson • 1992
Aristophanes: The Birds • Jeffrey Henderson • 1999
Aristophanes: Clouds • Jeffrey Henderson • 1992
Aristophanes: Lysistrata • Jeffrey Henderson • 1988
Aristophanes: Three Comedies: Acharnians, Lysistrata, Clouds • Jeffrey Henderson • 1997
Euripides: The Bacchae • Stephen Esposito • 1998
Euripides: Four Plays: Medea, Hippolytus, Heracles, Bacchae • Stephen Esposito, ed. • 2003
Euripides: Hecuba • Robin Mitchell-Boyask • 2006
Euripides: Heracles • Michael R. Halleran • 1988
Euripides: Hippolytus • Michael R. Halleran • 2001
Euripides: Medea • Anthony Podlecki • 2005, Revised
Euripides: The Trojan Women • Diskin Clay • 2005
Golden Verses: Poetry of the Augustan Age • Paul T. Alessi • 2003
Golden Prose in the Age of Augustus • Paul T. Alessi • 2004
Hesiod: Theogony • Richard Caldwell • 1987
The Homeric Hymns • Susan Shelmerdine • 1995
Ovid: Metamorphoses • Z. Philip Ambrose • 2004
Sophocles: Antigone • Ruby Blondell • 1998
Sophocles: King Oidipous • Ruby Blondell • 2002
Sophocles: Oidipous at Colonus • Ruby Blondell • 2003 Revised
Sophocles: Philoktetes • Seth Schein • 2003
Sophocles: The Theban Plays • Ruby Blondell • 2002
Terence: Brothers (Adelphoe) • Charles Mercier • 1998
Vergil: The Aeneid • Richard Caldwell • 2004

ISBN 978-0-941051-42-2
ISBN 10 0-941051-42-0

10 9 8 7 6 5

This book is published by Focus Publishing, R. Pullins & Company, Inc., PO Box 369, Newburyport MA 01950.

1207TS

Table of Contents

Preface

This reprint of the 1998 edition incorporates numerous corrections of typographical errors, minor revisions to the translation, and the like. The only important textual change to the translation itself regards the controversial choral refrain at 877-81 (=897-901). I have retranslated this passage in light of a discussion I had with the late Charles Segal. His argument for the proper understanding of this passage can now be found in his commentary (pp. 121-122) in *Euripides: Bakkhai* (Oxford, 2001) trans. Reginald Gibbons, notes and introduction by C. Segal.

In memory of my brother
Joseph
sit tibi terra levis

Plate 1. Mask of Dionysus (530 B.C.), neck amphora. Museo Nazionale, Tarquinia, Italy. Foto della Soprintendenza Archeologica per l'Etruria Meridionale.

Introduction

> I am really amazed that the scholastic nobility does not compre-
> hend his virtues, that they rank him below his predecessors, in the
> line with that high-toned tradition which the clown Aristophanes
> brought into currency.... Has any nation ever produced a dramatist
> who would deserve to hand him his slippers?
>
> Goethe on Euripides[1]

I. Introduction

Fifth-century Athens produced over nine hundred tragedies and six hundred fifty comedies. Of the forty-nine tragedians whose names we know,
we have the substantial remains of only three: Aeschylus (c. 525-456 B.C.),
Sophocles (c. 496-406) and Euripides (c. 484-406). This trio alone wrote some
three hundred plays, of which a scant thirty-two survive (seven, seven and
eighteen respectively) spanning the years 472 to 401 B.C. Fortunately Athenian tragedy, unlike the Athenian empire, ended with a bang not a whimper.
Euripides' last tragedy, the *Bacchae*, was produced posthumously (sometime
after 406 B.C.) by Euripides junior at the annual spring religious festival, the
'City Dionysia,' where nine tragedies and five comedies were staged over
several days in the massive Theater of Dionysus on the southern slope of the
Acropolis.[2] Sophocles' last tragedy, *Oedipus at Colonus*, was produced posthumously by the dramatist's grandson in 401. Both plays were written around
407/6, the year in which their authors died— but how very different their
visions, one heavy with human despair and divine vengeance, the other
uplifting with heroic inspiration and divine redemption as the gods sum-
mon the blind old Oedipus in rags, newly purified, into their company.

Euripides' *Bacchae* is arguably the darkest and most ferocious tragedy
ever written.[3] Its finale is one of those rare dramatic experiences that leaves
the spectator so completely frozen in horror and sadness that he can only
wonder if Gloucester was not right: "As flies to wanton boys are we to th'
gods, They kill us for their sport." (*King Lear* 4.1.36-37). An earthquake, a

---

1 Goethe (1831): quoted from B. Snell *The Discovery of the Mind: The Greek Origins of
European Thought* (1953) 135.
2 For evidence about the "City Dionysia" festival see *The Context of Ancient Drama*
(eds.) E. Csapo and W. Slater (1995) 103-21.
3 On 'absolute tragedy,' see G. Steiner 'Tragedy, Pure and Simple' in *Tragedy and the
Tragic* (ed.) M. Silk (1996) 534-46.

Plate 2. Dionysus dismembers a wild animal (450 B.C.), a stamnos from Vulci, Etruria. Copyright British Museum.

shattered palace, fits of madness, and the rending of animals by frenzied *maenads* ('mad women'),[4] a hilariously tragic cross-dressing scene, surreal visions of bulls and double suns, the tearing apart of an adolescent son by a maddened mother who then plays a game of ball with his body parts, the coaxing of that mother out of her insanity by her father, a merciless god coming 'out of the machine' to announce the undeserved fate of a loving grandfather who will be metamorphosed into a savage serpent: there are so many strange sequences, culminating in the destruction of the family (infanticide: Pentheus as son) and the city (regicide: Pentheus as king), that we are left groping for a stable center from which to understand this disturbing drama whose apocalyptic vision might well be said to symbolize the end of fifth-century Athens. More than any other Greek drama this one takes us deep into the heart of darkness.

One of the paradoxical beauties of Euripides' last tragedy is that it is simultaneously the most formally structured of all Greek dramas and the most violent in content. Its form just barely contains its chaos and terror. Where is Euripides taking us as we watch his effeminate god of ecstasy invade and explode, in rapid succession, the palace, the mind, and finally the body of King Pentheus? The relentless progression from political to

4 More information on words that are typed in italics, e.g. *maenads*, can be found in the Glossary.

psychological to physical fragmentation (*sparagmos*) makes us wonder how a divinity could be so vindictive.[5] Is there such wrath in heaven, and against an opponent so clearly outmatched? What is Euripides' message here, if there is one? Is Pentheus' opposition to the arrival of the new god and his cult a remake of earlier stories of crime and punishment by Euripides' predecessor Aeschylus? What are we to make of Dionysus in all this?[6] And is it accidental that the penultimate surviving Athenian tragedy is also the only one about the god whose fifteen-thousand seat theater stands at the

Plate 3. Maenad dancing (c. 490 B.C.), Attic drinking cup. Staatliche Antikensammlung, Munich, Germany. Foto Marburg/Art Resource, N.Y.

5 On this progression see C. Segal "The Menace of Dionysus: Sex Roles and Reversals in Euripides' *Bacchae*" in *Women in the Ancient World* (eds.) J. Peradotto and J. Sullivan (1984) 195-212.

6 In the short space of this introduction it is not possible to discuss the various aspects of Dionysus. For a fine up-to-date survey see A. Henrichs "Dionysus" in *The Oxford Classical Dictionary* 3rd ed. (eds.) S. Hornblower and A. Spawforth (1996) 479-82. On what makes Dionysus uniquely appropriate as the god of theater, see P. Easterling "A Show for Dionysus" in *The Cambridge Companion to Greek Tragedy* (ed.) P. Easterling (1997) 44-53; also Leinieks (1996) 351-61.

center of the city? Is it coincidence that Euripides, who produced some twenty-two sets of tetralogies over the span of half a century in Athens (455-406), wrote this one (apparently) from distant Macedonia in northern Greece at the court of King Archelaus? Is there any relationship between the ominous vision of this play, which won posthumously for the tragedian one of his rare first prizes (Euripides won four, Aeschylus thirteen, Sophocles eighteen), and the demise of the empire of Athens as a result of her struggle against Sparta in the Peloponnesian War (431-404 B.C.)? Where can we find firm ground on which to stand for a sense of perspective on these and related questions? In most tragedies we can look to the chorus because, even if they are not necessarily *the* voice of the city, they, being Greeks, usually provide a context of traditional Greek values, a moral compass by which we can orient ourselves. As an anonymous representative of the community the chorus usually embodies—from whatever their particular perspective (slave or free, male or female, old or young, maiden or married, citizen or suppliant)—some aspect of the city's conservative and established customs (*nomos*). Their precepts often cluster around virtues like prudent thinking and moderation, virtues extolled by such Delphic proverbs as "Know thyself" and "Nothing in excess." And so it is with the chorus of Bacchae. Through much of the play, despite the fact that they are foreigners from Asia and frenzied female devotees of the god Bacchus, they praise piety, lawfulness, happiness, tranquility, tradition, and moderation. But it is also true that this Asian chorus grows more vengeful (following the lead of their god) as the play progresses, so that after Pentheus' final departure we hear them sing "Let sword-bearing justice go forth, slaying Pentheus right through the throat" (993-95) and "Go, Bacchus, and with a laughing face cast the noose of death on the hunter of the Bacchae" (1020-23). This ambivalent mixture of attitudes makes it difficult to use the chorus as our interpretive guide, at least initially. On what solid ground, then, can we stand? Perhaps the best starting place is the structuring of the events themselves, since, as Aristotle declared (*Poetics* ch. 6), plot-structure is "the first principle and soul of tragedy."

II. The plot of the *Bacchae*

The god Dionysus, disguised as an effeminate long-haired young man, enters alone and explains to the audience that he has returned home after spreading his mystic rites across Asia. He will establish his divinity and cult in Thebes and use the city as his base for conquering Greece. He has come first to this city because it is his place of birth and because he wants to avenge the *hybris* (insolence) of his mother's three sisters (Agave, Autonoe, Ino), who have refused to accept the fact of his divine birth from the mortal Semele and the immortal Zeus. These three daughters of Cadmus (founder and former king of Thebes) claimed that it was some mortal man, not Zeus, who made their sister pregnant. In anger Dionysus has driven all

Plate 4. Maenad dismembers a wild animal (450 B.C.), amphora. Bibliothéque Nationale, Paris.

the women of the city into a frenzy and onto Mt. Cithaeron where, in three cult groups (*thiasoi*) led by the trio of sisters, they have been forcefully initiated into the Dionysiac mysteries by being transformed into *maenads* or *Bacchae* who worship the god with their ecstatic songs and dances.

King Pentheus, the adolescent son of Agave, outraged by reports of orgiastic female activity on the mountain, has arrested and jailed as many of the Bacchae as he could capture. He is also hunting down the Stranger from Asia, "quack dealer in spells" and leader of the *maenads*, on charges of corrupting the women of Thebes and driving them from their homes and hybristically claiming that Dionysus is a god. The blind old prophet Tiresias, dressed up as a *maenad* and sounding more like a sophistic word merchant than the venerable seer familiar from Sophocles' earlier *Antigone* and *Oedipus Rex*, tries to convince Pentheus that Dionysus, as the inventor of wine, is a force of nature who should be accepted. He is joined by Cadmus, Pentheus' grandfather, who is also magically rejuvenated with religious enthusiasm and ready to dance for the god. Cadmus argues that even if Dionysus is not a real god, Pentheus would be "lying for a good cause," namely family honor, by saying that Semele gave birth to an immortal. This aged pair of pedantic conventionalists only make the tempestuous Pentheus more angry.[7] Ensconced in his hearsay knowledge, youthful ar-

---

7 On the difficulty of assessing Cadmus and Tiresias, see S. Goldhill, "Doubling and Recognition in the *Bacchae*," *Metis* 3 (1988) 137-56.

rogance, and narrow-mindedness, Pentheus will have none of "this latest god, Dionysus, whoever he is." He orders his men to arrest the Asian Stranger; decapitation will be the punishment.

Confronted with the intransigent resistance of this 'fighter against the gods' (*theo-machos*), whose characteristic *modus operandi* for solving problems is the use of force, Dionysus, disguised as the Asian 'Stranger,' presents a series of miracles designed to reveal his godhead and convince Pentheus of his folly. These miracles, which become gradually more explicit as revelations of the god's divinity, include the mysterious escape of the *maenads* from jail, the supernatural events at the palace (the earthquake that shakes Pentheus' palace, the bursting forth of fire from Semele's tomb, the liberation of the Stranger from his chains), the macabre rending of beasts by the *maenads* on the mountain, and their routing of local armies of men and sacking of local villages.

These uncanny manifestations of divine power only make Pentheus more determined to put an end to this Bacchic madness. His mind has no room for the mysterious and miraculous. He is a imperious monarch who will use force to save his city from this destructive threat. Dionysus, therefore, is compelled to abandon the first device for proving his divinity (i.e., driving all the Theban women onto the mountain in a frenzy) and adopt a new plan (i.e., driving the king himself onto the mountain in a frenzy, 811-48). Pentheus, having been placed under Dionysus' spell, comes out of the palace dressed as "a woman, a *maenad*, a bacchant" and immediately undergoes an extraordinary transformation: he sees two suns and two cities and the Stranger as a horned bull. Dionysus easily convinces the frenzied Pentheus, in his effeminate costume, to journey to Mt. Cithaeron to spy on his mother and her *maenads*. Decked out with his *thyrsus* (a long, ivy-crowned fennel stalk which the god could endow with magical power) and fawnskin dress, he is ready to ascend the mountain, escorted by the Stranger, eager to be cradled in his mother's arms.

The horrific events that transpire on Cithaeron are reported by one of the king's slaves. While Pentheus was spying on the *maenads* from his hiding place atop a tall fir tree, they, incited by Dionysus to take revenge, espied him and uprooted the tree. Intent on passively observing what he thinks is sexual and drunken behavior by the Bacchae, Pentheus now becomes an animal victim torn to pieces by his mother, "the sacred priestess of the slaughter," "blessed Agave" who was "wisely urged on by the wise hunter Bacchus." Pentheus the hunter and the spectator has suddenly become the hunted and the spectacle as Agave, the mad bacchant, believing that she has captured a lion, impales her son's head on her *thyrsus*. Triumphantly this mother-turned-hunter returns from mountain to city, bringing the savagery of that wilderness with her. Covered in the blood of her

Plate 5. Maenad and Satyr (c. 490 B.C.), Attic amphora. Staatliche Antikensammlungen, Munich, Germany. Foto Marburg/Art Resources, N.Y.

prey, she is eager to have her son affix this trophy as a dedication on the frieze over the central door of his palace. Boasting of her great victory, Agave invites her father Cadmus and all of Thebes to share in "the feast" that will consume the body of the beast she has killed.

In the first 'psychotherapy scene' in Western literature, the bereft Cadmus, who has just returned from the mountain where he gathered together the mangled pieces of the grandson to whom he had entrusted his kingship, coaxes his daughter back to sanity as she unknowingly cradles her son's head in her arms. She soon realizes, in one of the most hair-raising 'recognition' scenes in tragedy, that the head she is holding does not belong to a lion. Apparently at this point the stage action included an assembly of Pentheus' body parts (a large gap in the text prevents certainty). Both Agave and Cadmus lament over the young man, the latter delivering a funeral oration over his grandson's corpse. Then, quite unexpectedly, atop the palace roof, Dionysus appears for the first time as a god (*deus ex machina*) and makes a bizarre prophecy: Cadmus and his wife Harmonia will go into exile and become rulers of a barbarian tribe that will destroy many cities; later they will be transformed into savage serpents and still later will reach the land of the blessed. Agave and her sisters will be exiled to another land. It is possible but not certain that Dionysus also announced the establishment of his cult in Thebes (1329-51; this section, too, is marred by a serious textual gap). All these prophecies of Dionysus are in accord with the will and oracle of his father Zeus. The two battered humans, Cadmus and Agave, father and daughter, embrace and then presumably depart in opposite directions after Agave renounces the cult of Dionysus.

III. Formal Elements and Structural Design

Euripides' plot probably follows closely the traditional outline of the myth about Dionysus' return home and his revenge on Pentheus. This story had been set forth at least as early as Aeschylus' lost trilogy on the subject (about which we know very little although it probably included a *Bacchae* and *Pentheus*). The plot's main components are Dionysus' arrival and introduction of his rites; resistance to the god, with arguments pro and con; direct confrontation between Dionysus as 'the Stranger' and Pentheus; and the king's madness and death. There is a clear progression from beginning (exposition) to middle (confrontation) to end (aftermath). The parts are causally connected so as to set forth a logical unity.[8]

This linear progression is enhanced by another striking unity, namely the chronological presentation of main characters which proceeds in a circular or chiastic pattern.[9] This highly symmetrical 'ring structure' seems deliberately designed to give us another perspective from which to comprehend the chaos of the action. We see Dionysus as a mortal in disguise and Dionysus as an immortal without disguise framing the play in the prologue and epilogue. Between these two poles the action will play itself out as Pentheus is transformed from hunter to hunted, spectator to spectacle, man to woman, authoritative king to sacrificial scapegoat. The three consecutive confrontations at the plot's center illustrate the ironic pattern of the play as a whole, proceeding from the apparent defeat of the Stranger as he is jailed by Pentheus (Act 2), to the psychic capture of Pentheus as he

---

8 The plot of the *Bacchae* can be outlined as follows [cp. O. Taplin (1978) 157]:
   a) 1-433: *Preparation for confrontation:* situation in Thebes
      1. Dionysus' homecoming and introduction of his rites (Prologue:1-63)
      2. conversion of Tiresias and Cadmus (Act 1: 170-369)
   b) 434-976: *Confrontation:* resistance to the god (Pentheus vs. the Stranger)
      1. confrontation #1: apparent defeat of the Stranger (Act 2: 434-518)
      2. confrontation #2: psychic capture of Pentheus (Act 3: 576-861)
      3. confrontation #3: decisive victory of the Stranger (Act 4: 912-976)
   c) 977-1392: *Result of confrontation:* fates of Pentheus, Agave, and Cadmus
      1. killing of Pentheus by Agave (Act 5: 1024-1152)
      2. Agave's madness and recovery; Dionysus' verdict (Epilogue: 1165-1392)
9 The actors appear in the following symmetrical ring pattern:
      a. Dionysus: god, disguised as man, describes his mission (Prologue)
      b. Tiresias/Cadmus: innocuous consequences of maenadism (Act 1)
      c. Pentheus: hunter of maenads (Act 1)
      d. Stranger: defeated by Pentheus [appearance] (Act 2)
      e. Pentheus: man as woman: cross-dressing (Act 3)
      d. Stranger: defeats Pentheus [reality] (Act 4)
      c. Pentheus: hunted by maenads, via report of messenger (Act 5)
      b. Agave/Cadmus: lethal consequences of maenadism (Epilogue)
      a. Dionysus: god, undisguised, on mission accomplished (Epilogue)
   I have borrowed the basic scheme from T. Webster *Greek Art and Literature, 500-430 B.C.* (1939) 159.

Plate 6. Maenad with penis and tail dances before Dionysus (400 B.C.), Interior of Attic red-figure kylix. Corinth Museum, Corinth, Greece. Courtesy American School of Classical Studies at Athens, Corinth Excavations; photographers I. Ioannidou and L. Bartziotou.

is coaxed into cross-dressing by the Stranger (Act 3), to the decisive victory of the Stranger over Pentheus with his frenzied double vision (Act 4). Euripides has bracketed the major confrontation of Act 3 (286 lines) with the much shorter Acts 2 and 4 (75 and 65 lines respectively). Like a movie director the dramatist uses his camera to frame and illuminate the crucial dramatic sequences. Even so brief an analysis begins to show us how Euripides has blocked his play structurally, ever so steadily zeroing in on the fierce struggle between man and god that is the heart of the *Bacchae*. What is at stake is the control of the city, the control of the women, the control of Pentheus' psyche, and indeed the control of the plot itself.[10] But the issue is not only who has the power but what constitutes power.

IV. Major themes

Euripides' play presents two radically divergent views of power brought into violent collision with one another. These differing perspectives are symbolized most clearly by the drama's two dominant physical spaces, the city and the mountain. The city embodies civilization in its most articulate shape. It is a place of culture whose walls protect it from the unruly outside world of nature, beasts, and barbarians. In the Greek imagination the city is (ideally) a place of order, wisdom, sanity, cooked (as opposed to

10 See F. Zeitlin *Playing the Other: Gender and Society in Classical Greek Literature* (1996) 360-61.

raw) food, architecture, law, morality, religion, and politics. Certainly that is not what Pentheus' city embodies, but he *thinks* it does and for the play that is important. Most of all, Pentheus' Thebes, with its mighty walls and palace prisons, is a bastion of the male warrior code. He personifies that code and rules the city accordingly—with a fierce temper and an iron fist. When a problem arises, his customary response is to hunt, capture, arrest, bind with chains, and imprison the enemy.

Beyond the severe walls and tight-fisted regulations of Pentheus' seven-gated city is the wilderness of the mountain, Cithaeron, where Dionysus has driven mad all the women of Thebes. Euripides' schematization could not be more emphatic: the males occupy the city, the females the mountain. What happens in one arena is the opposite of what happens in the other.[11] If Thebes is city and law (*nomos*), Cithaeron is anti-city and nature (*physis*). The mountain embodies that which is beyond human control; it is linked to the city only by boundary-crossing characters such as shepherds and herdsmen; and, of course, by Dionysus, the boundary transgressor *par excellence*. The mountain in the *Bacchae* is the kingdom of nature and all its green energy, the place of *maenads* with their song, dance, ecstasy, fawnskins, madness, disorder, and miracles. The audience never sees this world of exotic otherness since it is miles from Thebes but Euripides brings it to brilliant life in the huge orchestra ('dancing circle') where the *Asian* Bacchae, visible to the audience, are decked out in their animal costumes and ivy wreaths. They are mirror images of the *Theban* Bacchae on Mt. Cithaeron, who are invisible to the audience, but similarly dressed. The choral song and dance of the Asian Bacchae, vigorously driven by the pounding rhythms of their oriental drums, transports to the city the mountain world of the Theban Bacchae. But the choral songs are not only bacchic and exuberant; they are often reflections on, and celebrations of, traditional Greek wisdom and warnings about the perils of *hybris* and the transgression of divine law.

This peculiar duality within the chorus—one part nature, another part culture; one part Asian, another part Greek; one part fierce and vengeful, another part peaceful and gentle—mingles the worlds of mountain and city.[12] It finds an analogue not only in the duality of Dionysus but also in Pentheus. Despite all his head-strong maleness there is a part of him that wants to participate in, or rather peer into, this other world represented by the frenzied women on the mountain. He has an *erôs* (813), a strong desire, to see the *maenads*, and especially his mother, on Cithaeron. But that sexual passion collides with his masculine sense of honor and glory. He would

---

11 See R. Friedrich "City and Mountain: Dramatic Spaces in Euripides' *Bacchae*" *Proceedings of the XIIth Congress of the International Comparative Literature Association* vol. 2 *Space and Boundaries in Literature* (1988) 538-45.

12 On the radical, anti-civic spirit of the Asian *maenads* see C. Segal "Chorus and Community in Euripides' *Bacchae*" in *Poet, Public, and Performance in Ancient Greece* (eds.) L. Edmunds and R. Wallace (1997) 65-86.

Plate 7. Initiation into the Dionysiac Mysteries (60 B.C.), wall-painting from the Villa of Mysteries, Pompeii. Alinari/Art Resource, N.Y.

not be 'caught dead' dressed as a woman; yet that is the only way he can spy on them. The vehemence with which he rejects the feminine suggests an insecurity about his own sexuality. But it is important to remember that Pentheus is probably only about eighteen years old. He knows virtually nothing about sex and not much more about life. Why should he? His father Echion ('Snake-man'), born from the dragon's teeth sown by Cadmus and so bypassing birth from the female, is absent from his life (and, largely, from the play). His mother Agave, leader of the *maenads*, has become the enemy in that other place. It is true that Pentheus has a surrogate father in his grandfather Cadmus, but the old man is hardly a paradigm of fatherhood or political authority, all bedecked in his Bacchic dress and headed off to the mountain to dance. His lesson about family is that Pentheus should accept the new god Dionysus, even if it means lying, so that the house of Cadmus can accrue more honor.

The lack of parental role models means that Pentheus is unschooled in life and in one of its most baffling mysteries, namely sexuality. Some critics call him a Peeping Tom or a perverted voyeur. But these characterizations can be taken too far or, more dangerously, isolate the tragedy's themes to one young man's narrow perspective. Pentheus is what he is, an adolescent struggling to become a man and a king. And his struggle must be read in context. Pentheus' suspicions about the nocturnal drunkenness and promiscuity of the *maenads*, based on reports delivered to him while he was out of the country, are not without some basis. He has, after all, returned home to a city out of control. The whole situation is sexually charged: women driven mad onto a mountain, at night, with wine, worshipping some exotic foreigner. Tiresias tells Pentheus that Dionysus will not force the *maenads* to be chaste, though the truly virtuous ones will be (317-18). This opens the possibility that those *maenads* who are not really self-controlled might be corrupted. No wonder Pentheus is concerned. What inexperienced young Greek king would not be? In the context of late fifth-century Athenian culture, Pentheus' fear is even more understandable. *Maenads*, after all, had a reputation. Their sexual activity was omni-present on Greek vases; satyrs, the phallic followers of Dionysus, were forever pursuing them. In a fragment of Aeschylus (448) *maenads* are called "shameless [i.e. loose] women." And Euripides' *Ion* (c. 410 B.C.) speaks of them at the wine-god's torch-lit festival atop Mt. Parnassus in the context of drunkenness and sex.

A similar perspective can be taken on the issue of Pentheus as 'a fighter against the gods' as he is called by the Stranger, Tiresias and Agave. It is important to note that Pentheus is not alone in his opposition to the new so-called god. The entire city of Thebes, both women and men, rejected Dionysus, all except Cadmus and Tiresias (195), whose motives for believing are hardly theologically inspiring. Like *maenads*, 'new gods' had a reputation. Late fifth-century Athens was teeming with foreigner mercenaries and slaves as a result of the Peloponnesian War. This invasion of foreigners meant an influx of numerous new divinities and mystery cults; these were often the target of the comic poets. One of these new gods was Sabazius, an oriental version of Dionysus from the mountains of Phrygia (Asia Minor) and Thrace (northern Greece). His Dionysus-like cult included nocturnal rituals, ecstatic dances and music (flute and kettledrum), and animals (snakes, bulls, fawn) which served as vehicles of the god. Cicero tells us that "In one of his plays Aristophanes, the wittiest poet of Old Comedy, so satirized the new gods and the nightlong observances of their rites, that Sabazius and certain other gods, having been condemned as foreigners, were thrown out of the city."[13] The point of citing the preceding evidence is to suggest that, in the context of Euripides' world, Pentheus' fears about the promiscuity of the *maenads* and his hostility to the cult of the 'new god' are not so outlandish as critics sometimes make them seem.

Pentheus, then, as he attempts to negotiate the rite of passage from adolescence to manhood, does the best he can with the little he has. To dramatize the perils of this rite of passage, Euripides uses initiation into the mysteries of Dionysus as his vehicle. Why Dionysus? Because he is the god

---

13 Cicero *On the Laws* 2.15; the comedy in question seems to be Aristophanes' lost *Seasons*, probably produced between 423 and 408.

Plate 8. Pentheus dismembered by Maenads (A.D. 62), wall-painting from the House of Vetti, Pompeii. Alinari/Art Resource, N.Y.

who challenges and confounds all the rigid dichotomies of Pentheus' life. Dionysus is both mortal and immortal, god and beast, Greek and Asian, gentle and savage, playful and violent, calm and frenzied, comic and tragic, born of male and female wombs (Zeus' and Semele's), inhabitant of the city and of the mountain, initiator into the life of his mysteries and conductor into Hades of those who resist initiation. These are some of the polarities contained within Dionysus himself. From a perspective that looks outward rather than inward, Dionysus (god of theater, mask, madness, wine, and illusion) represents the antithesis of Apollo (god of rationality, restraint, consciousness, light, and order.)[14] Perhaps for this reason the Athenians

14 See F. Nietzsche *The Birth of Tragedy* (1872), esp. sections 1-5; on the Dionysiac *Bacchae* as Euripides' refutation of Aeschylus' Apollonian *Oresteia* trilogy, see C. Paglia *Sexual Personae: Art and Decadence from Nefertiti to Emily Dickinson* (1990) 88-109.

situated the Theater of Dionysus at the center of their community. The city, with all its rage for order, is basically Apollonian. But beneath the cultural constructs which make up civilization is a 'subterranean something' that must be incorporated into the city; thus at the end of Aeschylus' *Oresteia* trilogy (458 B.C.), Athena, goddess of the city, understands that somehow she must persuade the ancient Furies, powers of the earth and defenders of the ghost of slain Clytemnestra, to become part of the city. That 'subterranean something' which pulses through both cities and individuals, "the force that through the green fuse drives the flower" (Dylan Thomas' phrase), that is Dionysus, at once most gentle and most terrifying for mankind. Like the intoxicating wine of which he is god, Bacchus is the liquid force of liberation who allows mortals to free themselves from the restrictions and boundaries that culture must inevitably create to sustain itself.

If Dionysus is the god of liberation, what does he liberate in the *Bacchae*? One of the most eminent scholars of Euripides has recently argued that Dionysus liberates Thebes politically from the oppressive autonomous rule of Pentheus and "the *irredeemably* self-destructive rejection of the god by the *royal family*"; that the god, in his final epiphany, establishes himself and his cult (this must remain uncertain because of a textual gap) as a vital and cohesive force for the benefit of the city.[15] This thesis simply does not tally with the emotional experience of the tragedy as a whole and certainly not with the final scene. Could a mother cradling her own son's head, a head that *she* severed, welcome this god's cult? Or a grandfather reassembling the corpse of his grandson? If this is a god bringing cohesion to a city, who could want such a god? Speaking to Dionysus about this excessive punishment Cadmus complains (1348): "Gods ought not be like mortals in their *passions (orgê)*." It is precisely this, the god's vengeful *passion*, that reverberates through the epilogue. His wrath has shattered the city and its people—politically, psychologically and physically. That is how Cadmus and Agave see it. Nowhere does the text suggest that Pentheus' death will lead to the salvation of Thebes. The dramatist highlights human desolation, not civic liberation.

Why, then, is Dionysus so vindictive and why does the *Bacchae* end so darkly? A more convincing thesis is that Euripides is presenting a radical critique of the city in which he produced tragedies for half a century.[16] Looking down from Macedonia in northern Greece, where he seems to have exiled himself around 408 B.C. (presumably in frustration at the sad state of affairs in Athens), what Euripides saw was an Athenian 'tragedy' writ large. What kind of city would paint Pentheus into a corner, or allow

---

15 See R. Seaford *Euripides' Bacchae* (1996) 47 ff.; although I disagree with Seaford's general interpretation, it will be clear from my notes how much I have learned from his commentary, esp. with regard to the play's allusions to the Dionysiac mysteries.

16 See the brilliant essay of W. Arrowsmith "A Greek Theater of Ideas" in *Ideas in the Drama* (ed.) J. Gassner (1964) 1-41.

Plate 9. Roman Senate's decree suppressing worship of Bacchus in 186 B.C.
Courtesy Kunsthistorisches Museum, Vienna. (See Appendix Four for discussion.)

Pentheus to paint himself into a corner, where his choices were constrained by such narrow cultural constructions of right and wrong, where the dichotomies of gender had become so rigid and isolating as to invite fragmentation of community and of self [17] ("Indeed you, Pentheus, are the only one who toils for this city, the only one!" 963), where *erôs* had become so divorced from *sophia* (wisdom) that young men like Pentheus, virtually devoid of role models, were bound to become a union of card-carrying misfits who knew neither themselves nor their world?

Euripides as culture critic personifies the poet as prophet.[18] His *Medea*

---

17 Cp. Segal (note 5) 197 on the consequences of Pentheus' male-dominated perspective: "This society's extreme sexual differentiation, even with its preferential treatment of the masculine, is as inimical to male as to female psychic integration. The women become mad and leave the inner space which defines them and gives them their secure, if limited, identity; yet the men too suffer dismemberment."

18 See B. Knox "Euripides: The Poet as Prophet" in *Directions in Euripidean Criticism* (ed.) P. Burian (1985) 1-12.

(431 B.C.), along with *Hippolytus* (428) on the one hand, and *Orestes* (408), *Iphigeneia at Aulis* (406), and *Bacchae* (406) on the other, virtually frame the years of the Peloponnesian War (431-404). These plays bracket the tearing apart of a once magnificent culture, a city that had, in time past, harmoniously yoked passion and wisdom (see *Medea* 824-45). The prophetic *Medea* dramatized *erôs* unbound, passion gone crazy: a mother forced to choose between love for her children and lust for revenge on a husband who had abandoned her for a younger and politically more advantageous bride. Euripides here problematizes the age-old Greek moral code of "help your friends, hurt your enemies": what happens when the enemy is in your own house? Since, by Greek cultural definition, revenge against the enemy provided the surest path to attaining glory, Medea, like a Greek hoplite warrior, armed her heart in steel (1242) and murdered her two boys. She would prove to her husband who was more powerful. The outraged Jason confidently proclaims that "there is no Greek woman who would have dared such a deed" (1339). We are meant to doubt him; for he has failed to understand that "great suffering makes a stone of the heart" (Yeats). When, in the shocking finale, this mother-turned-monster flies off in the chariot of the Sun god, the personification of pollution being whisked off by the symbol of purity, we see *Erôs* unbound headed for Athens. The fifth-century historian Thucydides, who chronicled so brilliantly the first two decades of the Athens-Sparta debacle, describes how the kind of *erôs* personified by Medea arrived in Athens. In recounting the Athenian decision to sail on the ill-fated Sicilian expedition in 415-413 B.C., Thucydides says "All alike fell in love (*erôs*) with the enterprise.... With this enthusiasm of the majority, the few that liked it not, feared to appear unpatriotic by holding up their hands against it, and so kept quiet."[19] The casualty list of that expedition: seven thousand Athenians captured, thousands killed, and over one hundred warships destroyed. *Erôs* had indeed gone crazy. Euripides revisited this theme often but nowhere more bitterly than in 407/6 B.C. (he died in the spring of that year). In *Iphigeneia at Aulis*, one of the plays of the *Bacchae* tetralogy, Achilles speaks of "the terrible passion (*deinos erôs*, 808) that has fallen upon Greece for this expedition [to Troy] not without the gods' [prompting]." Similarly Agamemnon describes how "some Aphrodite has driven the Greek army mad with desire for sailing as quickly as possible against the barbarians" (1263). In the face of this military madness the only salvation was the hero-

---

19 *Thucydides: The Peloponnesian War* 6.24 trans. R. Crawley (1876; Modern Library reprint 1951). For the theme compare Thucydides (3.84) on the civil war at Corcyra in 427 B.C. where the breakdown of law was so severe that fathers were killing their own sons. The historian speaks "of the savage and pitiless excesses into which men who had begun the struggle not in a class but in a party spirit, were hurried by their ungovernable *passions (orgê)*. In the confusion into which life was now thrown in the cities, human nature, always rebelling against the law and now its master, gladly showed itself ungoverned in *passion (orgê)*...."

ism of a teenage girl, unpracticed in the politics of mob rule, willing to sacrifice herself for her country. Maybe, just maybe, the demagogues and buck-passing generals might learn from the courage of Iphigeneia.

What has all this to do with the *Bacchae*? The *Bacchae*, along with *Orestes* and *Iphigeneia at Aulis*, looks back to the themes of the earlier *Medea* and *Hippolytus*. The *erôs* that flew out of Corinth winging towards Athens at the end of *Medea* all those years ago has here finally reached its destination, further twisted and distorted by its twenty-five year journey through the intervening Peloponnesian War, the "violent teacher" that revealed to all Greece the many faces of atrocity (Thuc. 3.82). It might seem that *erôs* has little part in the *Bacchae* since the word appears only once (813). But the *erôs* for revenge that once consumed Medea—the damsel in distress transformed into semi-divine Fury—and the *erôs* for revenge that once consumed Aphrodite and Artemis in *Hippolytus*, that passion now consumes Dionysus: "Pentheus will come to the Bacchae and pay the penalty of death....Let us punish him! ... I want the Thebans to mock him" (848-54); "Take revenge on him!" (1081). It was this god who "gave special ease to her hands" as

Plate 10. Christ as Dionysus, cathedral door-handle in Güstrow, Germany (13th-14th c.). Courtesy William Calder.

Agave, "foaming at the mouth..., held fast by the Bacchic god," ripped out her son's shoulder (1124-28). Despite their different modes of operation (effeminate Asian guile vs. masculine Greek force), these two first cousins, Dionysus and Pentheus, share a similar passion for honor and power. Dionysus *will* establish his godhead with a vengeance and punish any resistance; Pentheus *will* govern his city with an iron fist and punish any resistance. Why does Euripides present such a conflict of divine and human 'wills to power' as the crux of his play? In part to reveal Dionysus as a divine power, a natural force within the human psyche that must be honored, respected, and indeed celebrated. When denied, as in the case of Pentheus, this force will erupt with volcanic fury. That explains part of Dionysus' taurine ferocity. But Euripides meant to extend that private, familial theme to the public, political arena as well. In other words, the tragedy of the self implied the tragedy of the city. And that meant exposing, through the theme of revenge, the brutal reality of power politics in the late fifth century. "Of gods we believe and men we know that by a necessary law of their nature, they rule wherever they can." So the Athenians argued in 415 B.C. before they massacred all the men of military age on the island of Melos (Thucydides 5. 105). It was not an argument that left any room for compassion. Euripides presents in his protagonist and antagonist some of the ugly facts of the Peloponnesian War; Dionysus and Pentheus seem to embody the anger of jealous imperial city-states battling one another.[20] If there is no clear moral center in the mythic world of the *Bacchae* that is because there is no clear moral center in the contemporary world of Euripides. The *Bacchae*, like so much of Euripides, presents fragments of characters. Medea, Hippolytus, Agave, Pentheus: they are all just parts of a whole. The old Sophoclean protagonist, bound to a Promethean rock of moral certitude, had little purchase on Euripides because that kind of heroic temper had disappeared from his everyday world.

The collision of the two 'wills to power' in the *Bacchae* gradually reveals a chink in Pentheus' breast-plate of bravura, an ambivalent erotic passion (813) that had hitherto disguised itself as angry authority. Once released, this Dionysiac *erôs*, manifested as the Bacchic bull (618, 920), so completely overwhelms the adolescent Pentheus that he becomes, in his quest for the forbidden knowledge of the Aphrodisiac activity of the Bacchae, "the suffering one" that his Greek name indicates. In similar fashion a savage bull had risen miraculously up out of a "supernatural wave" and destroyed Hippolytus, a young man who thought, like Pentheus, that he had everything, including his sexuality, under control (*Hipp.* 1203-47).[21] In that ear-

---

20 See B. Knox "Divine Intervention in Euripidean Thought" in *Studi di Filologia Classica in Onore di Giusto Monaco* vol. 1 (1991) 223-30.

21 On the sexual significance of the bull see C. Segal "Pentheus and Hippolytus on the Couch and on the Grid: Psychoanalytic and Structuralist Readings of Greek Tragedy" in *Interpreting Greek Tragedy: Myth, Poetry, Text* (1986) 268-93.

lier play (428 B.C.) the bull, whose virile image is manifestly sexual, was set loose by the vengeful curse of Hippolytus' father, Theseus, and found its physical manifestation in the sacred tidal wave sent by Theseus' father, the Earth-Shaker Poseidon. In the *Bacchae* the bull is let loose by the avenger, Dionysus, who summons "the august goddess of Earthquakes" to shatter Pentheus' palace. This 'palace miracle' was just a warning to the king. But when the warning was ignored the bull had to return ever more ferociously. That it should return as madness incarnate in the name of the mother may well be the most savage irony in the tragic corpus. "Father," Agave proclaims, "now you can boast most proudly that you, of all mortals, have sown by far the best daughters" (1233-34). So indeed she has realized, like her son, the Greek meaning of her name, "the illustrious one."

Euripides' earlier prophetic warnings were history now. The pathetic image of a Bacchic mother, driven mad by the angry son of god the father, raising the impaled head/mask of her own son on a cultic *thyrsus* in honor of the god of liberation, this horrific image was Euripides' final vision. Night had fallen. Now was a time for pity and fear. It was too late for anything else; too late for Pentheus and Agave, too late for Athens, and even too late, it seems, for the genre of tragedy itself, with its stage building shattered, its protagonist torn to pieces, and its royal mask disembodied by the theater god's most zealous devotee.[22]

A Note to the Reader

This edition has many footnotes, appendices, and a full glossary. More than other Greek tragedies, this play requires a knowledge of historical and religious material which the average reader cannot be expected to know. This said, I strongly urge the reader *to read the play first* with as little reference to the footnotes as possible. After all, "the play's the thing." The notes are there for subsequent study. (The more important ones have been put in bold type.) In the notes and glossary I often quote certain scholars (Dodds, Taplin, Seaford, and Leinieks) because their observations on this complex tragedy are so illuminating but not generally accessible. For the same reason I have quoted other scholars as seemed appropriate. I regret that I have

---

22 "... too late for Athens." In 405-404 B.C. after their final defeat by Sparta at Aegospotami in the Hellespont (northeastern Aegean Sea), the Athenians saw their empire destroyed. After 395 B.C. the city would regain some of her power but in 405-404 Athens was financially exhausted and starved into submission; portions of the city's walls were razed; three thousand Athenians had been executed at Aegospotami and one hundred Athenian warships had been captured or destroyed in that battle (Sparta eventually allowed her to keep twelve ships); democracy was then briefly abolished, and the council of thirty oligarchs began their reign of terror. On all this see Plutarch *Life of Lysander* ch.11-15 and Xenophon *Hellenica* 2.1-3. Tragedy, like democracy, would continue in the fourth century but it was a pale shadow of its predecessor; see P. Easterling "The end of an era? Tragedy in the early fourth century" in *Tragedy, Comedy, and the Polis* (eds.) Jeffrey Henderson *et al.* (1993) 559-69.

not been able to acknowledge all those whose work I have incorporated; space precluded that luxury. But anyone who works on this play realizes that he stands on the shoulders of many outstanding predecessors. The translation has aimed at staying close to the letter of Euripides' ancient Greek text, and to the spirit as well. Translations from Greek and Latin are my own unless otherwise indicated. Errors are also, of course, my own. Further study resources for students, teachers, and general readers are available on the internet at *http://www.pullins.com/excerpts/bacchae/ bacchae.htm*. These will be updated and expanded, but for now include: Appendix One: The lacuna after line 1300: Agave's lament; Appendix Two: The lacuna after line 1329. (These two appendices are expansions of the first two appendices in the present volume.); Appendix Three: Three outlines of the *Bacchae*; Appendix Four: Outlines of several key speeches and scenes in the *Bacchae*; Appendix Five: The Uniqueness of the *Bacchae*; Appendix Six: The Uniqueness of Dionysus; Appendix Seven: An extensive bibliography on the *Bacchae*. Further potential contributions are welcome; please send them to *espo@bu.edu*.

Acknowledgments

The Greek text I have followed for the most part is James Diggle's superb 1994 Oxford Classical Text of Euripides, volume 3. I would like to thank the following for their generous help: James Clauss and Michael Halleran, the readers for Focus Press; my scholarly friends Xavier Riu (Barcelona), Sarolta Takács (Harvard) and Keith Whitaker (Chicago); my colleagues at Boston University, John Carlevale, Jeffrey Henderson, Stephen Scully, and especially Jay Samons, for their constructive criticisms of my introduction. Charles Segal (Harvard), both in his scholarly work and in private communication, has been a source of inspiration, learning, and constructive criticism. Special thanks to my colleague Valerie Warrior for contributing her fine essay on "The Roman Bid to Control Bacchic Worship," which illustrates the historical importance, in the Roman world, of the problems raised by Euripides' play two centuries earlier, and to Wolfgang Haase for some suggestions therein. I also thank William Calder III for permission to publish the photograph in Plate 10 (taken by the late Dr. Wolfgang Schindler of the Winckelmann Institute, Humboldt Universität, Berlin).

I am very grateful to Cynthia Zawalich at Focus for her careful reading and to Ron Pullins, editor, for his patience, generosity, and expertise. My friend, Ilse Nehring, proofread the entire manuscript and has saved me from numerous errors. Over the years my many students in Greek Drama have taught me much about this amazing play; I thank them all. My dear friends Lewis Fried, Jameson Morris, Stephano Navarolli, Cindy Nelson, Mary Ann Sparks, and Daniel Weiner have been unwavering in their moral support. Lastly I must thank my parents, Mary and Joseph Esposito, for sustaining me with their abundant love. It is a humbling thing to be supported by so many; and a precious gift.

The Structural Division of the Play

Following modern convention, I have divided the play into 'acts,' using the six choral songs to define various episodes of action. (Adhering strictly to the structure of Greek tragedy, I would have defined the 'acts' by the comings and goings of characters. Modern convention is based on the five acts of Roman drama (Seneca), subsequently adopted by the Elizabethan playwrights of the 16th and 17th centuries.)

The Eight Characters and the Chorus

Agave: mother of Pentheus; daughter of Cadmus; sister of Autonoe, Ino, and Semele; leader of the Theban Bacchae; not on stage until 1168

Cadmus: grandfather of Pentheus and Dionysus; father of Agave; founder and former king of Thebes

Chorus: Fifteen Bacchae (frenzied female worshippers of Dionysus) from Lydia (in Asia Minor); also called 'maenads' (mad-women)

Dionysus (= 'The Stranger'): son of the immortal Zeus and the mortal Semele; first cousin of Pentheus; appears both as a god (1-63 and 1329-51) and as a human, i.e. as the disguised Lydian 'Stranger' (434-518, 604-861, 912-976)

Messenger #1: a herdsman from Thebes who describes (677-774) the miracles of the Theban Bacchae on Mt. Cithaeron

Messenger #2: one of Pentheus' slaves who describes (1043-1152) the tearing apart of his master by the Theban Bacchae

Pentheus: son of Agave and Echion; first cousin of Dionysus; successor to his grandfather Cadmus as king of Thebes; probably 18-20 years old

Soldier: one of Pentheus' guards who describes (434-50) how the Stranger was captured near Cithaeron and how the jailed Bacchae miraculously escaped to the mountain

Tiresias: the blind old prophet of Thebes and friend of Cadmus

Setting and Stage Directions

The time is the heroic past before the Trojan War, in the third generation after the founding of Thebes. The scene is the palace of King Pentheus on the acropolis of seven-gated Thebes, one of the most powerful cities of Mycenean Greece. Thebes was also a center of Dionysiac cult and a chief city of Boeotia ('Cow-land'), a region of central Greece; the city was dominated to the south by Mt. Cithaeron, some ten miles away.

The wooden facade of Pentheus' palace forms the back-drop at center stage and shows several Doric columns supporting an entablature (591, 1214). To one side is a fenced-in, vine-covered sanctuary containing the tomb of

21

Semele (Dionysus' mother) and the smouldering ruins of her house (7-12). Entrances and exits at stage left (from the spectator's viewpoint) represent arrivals and departures to and from the country and mountain (Cithaeron); those at stage right, to and from the city (Thebes). [For the reasons and problems behind this alignment see Glossary, 'Stage Directions.']

PROLOGUE°

[Enter Dionysus, stage left, disguised as an exotic young holy man from Asia; he carries a thyrsus,° wears a smiling mask, fawnskin cloak and ivy wreath. °]

Dionysus
I have come to this land of Thebes as the son of Zeus.°   1
Dionysus is my name.° Semele, the daughter of Cadmus,
gave me birth after being forced into labor by fiery lightning.
Exchanging my divinity for human form I have arrived
at Dirce's streams and the waters of Ismenus.°   5
I see the tomb of my thunder-struck mother here
near the palace and the fallen ruins of her house
smouldering with the still living flames of Zeus' blast,
a memorial of Hera's undying hybris° against my mother.°

Prologue's purpose (1-63): To convey immediately the necessary dramatic data. It is spoken by Dionysus in his character as a god and addressed only to the audience; the actors will not know that Dionysus is a god in disguise. The *Bacchae* is the sole surviving tragedy that presents a deity in mortal disguise. Opening speeches by gods are not so rare (four others in Euripides) but Euripidean gods generally do not interact with humans. The major exception is Dionysus.

Thyrsus: A long, light fennel-stalk crowned with a bundle of ivy. See Glossary, 'Thyrsus.'

Dionysus' appearance: In his disguise as the Stranger from Lydia he has an effeminate costume (453), long curly golden hair (235, 455, 493), fair skin (457), and ruddy cheeks (236). See Glossary, 'Dionysus.'

1: **Prologue's key-note**: The phrase 'the son of Zeus' emphasizes the speaker's divinity and implicitly challenges any opposition to that divinity.

2: A word-play on Dionysus' name: In the first two lines the Greek sequence *Dios...Dionysos* derives the name Dio-nysus from *Dios*, the possessive case of Zeus' name and thereby emphasizes the importance of Dionysus' descent from Zeus, king of the Olympian pantheon. See Glossary, 'Dionysus.'

5: Dirce and Ismenus: The two small rivers of Thebes, in the west and east quarters respectively. Dionysus was washed in the waters of Dirce at the time of his birth (cp. 519-22).

9: *Hybris* (wanton violence): Perhaps the play's most important word, this morally charged noun occurs more often in *Bacchae* than any other Greek tragedy (14 times, matched only by Sophocles' *Ajax*). *Hybris* is usually a deliberate act of violence against another person, meant to dishonor. See Glossary, 'Hybris.'

9: Hera's anger: The ruins of Semele's house are a memorial of the wrath of the queen of the gods. As Zeus' seventh and permanent wife, she was bitterly jealous of her husband's frequent affairs. Disguising herself as a human, Hera

I praise Cadmus who keeps this ground untrodden,   10
a shrine for his daughter. But it was I who covered her sanctuary
all around with the grape-vine's clustering foliage.°
After leaving the gold-rich fields of the Lydians
and Phrygians, I moved on to Persia's sun-parched plateaux
and Bactra's walls and the bleak land   15
of the Medes° and opulent Arabia
and all of Asia Minor whose parts hug the salty sea
with beautifully-towered cities
full of Greeks and barbarians mixed together.°
I first came to this Greek city   20
only after I had roused to dancing all those Asian lands
and established my rites there so that I might be seen by mortals as a
    god.°
It was this very Thebes, of all the Greek lands, that I first incited
to female shrieks of ecstasy, wrapping her in fawnskins,
putting into her hands the thyrsus, my ivy javelin.   25
I did this because my mother's sisters, of all people,°
denied that I, Dionysus, was begotten from Zeus. Semele, they say,
was seduced by some mortal but then, by Cadmus' clever contrivance,
she charged the error of her bed to Zeus. For this reason,
because Semele had lied about her union with the god,   30

---

persuaded her rival, Semele, to prevail upon Zeus to visit her in all his glory.
That meant Zeus had to appear with his thunder and lightning which in-
stantly incinerated Semele.

12: Semele's tomb: The seven lines of description at 6-12 point to the tomb's symbolic importance. The grapevine, which was Dionysus' sacred plant, marks
it as a holy place. The tomb's location is uncertain; probably it was on stage
(rather than in the orchestra) but off to the side, away from the acting area.
Burning incense would supply the smoke that rose from its eternal divine
flame (cp. 596-99, 623).

16: Medes: Inhabitants of Media, a mountainous country of Asia, southwest of the
Caspian Sea. Arabia's prosperity resulted from its wealth of exotic spices and
perfumes (Herodotus *History* 3.107).

13-19: **Dionysus' empire:** This geographic catalogue registers the huge extent
Dionysus' religious control. Nearly all of Asia (i.e. most of the Persian Empire) has *converted* to him, from coastal Asia Minor (Phrygia, Lydia) all the
way to Bactra, capital city of Bactria (gateway to India and China), some 3500
miles to the east. Having conquered the East, Dionysus will now conquer the
West, beginning with Thebes.

22: *Bacchae* as a play of revelation (cp. 42, 47-48, 182, 1031): Dionysus, having revealed himself to Asia, will now reveal himself to his native Thebes. He will do
so in two ways: by his presence on stage as a god and by the miracles through
which that presence keeps manifesting itself while he is disguised as a mortal.

26: Semele's sisters (= Dionysus' aunts): Agave, Autonoe, and Ino. See Glossary,
'Semele's sisters.'

her three sisters sneered that Zeus had killed her.°
To punish that slander I myself stung those same sisters,
hounding them from their homes with fits of frenzy so that now, °
knocked out of their senses, they make their homes on Mt. Cithaeron.°
I forced them to wear the vestments of my mysteries °   35
and the entire female seed of Cadmeians, all who were women,
I drove from their homes in madness.° Mingled together
with Cadmus' daughters, the women of Thebes sit beneath green firs
on roofless rocks.° For this city must learn well,
even if it doesn't want to learn,° that it is still uninitiated in my
       bacchic rites.°   40
I must vindicate my mother Semele
by revealing myself to mortals as the god whom she bore to Zeus.
       Cadmus, then, has passed the power and privileges of his monarchy
to the son of his daughter Agave. But that one, Pentheus,
fights against the gods by fighting against me.° He thrusts me away 45

26-31: **Denial of Dionysus' divinity:** This action by Semele's sisters impelled Dionysus
to drive them mad. They denied that it was *Zeus* who was Semele's partner.
Their account of events was as follows: a) that, in fact, Semele had become
pregnant by a mortal man (26-28); b) but that their father Cadmus, wishing to
protect his daughter's name by concealing her sexual 'error' (*hamartia*), con-
vinced Semele to lie and say that she had slept with Zeus, not some mortal (28-
29); and c) that Zeus, in anger at this lie, slew Semele (30-31; cp. 244).

33: **Dionysus as 'the god of frenzy':** The essence of this god-induced mania is ex-
travagant behavior whose manifestations include great agitation and violent
bodily movements. Dionysus stings the Bacchae here (cp. 119, 664, 979, 1229)
as horseflies sting cattle and excite a stampede (Leinieks 72, 87).

34: Cithaeron: A mountain sacred to Dionysus, ten miles south of Thebes. See Glossary, 'Mountains.'

35: **Forced worship:** A significant difference between the Theban Bacchae (offstage,
i. e. on Mt. Cithaeron) and the chorus of Asian Bacchae (in the orchestra) is
that the former are *involuntary* devotees (having been driven into a frenzy by
Dionysus) while the latter are, apparently, *voluntary* devotees.

32-37: **Dionysus' opening act of war:** This begins the play's action. All Thebes'
women are driven into a frenzy and onto the mountain. *The play, then, takes
place in a city without women* (except for the chorus of Asian maenads in the
orchestra) until Agave's entry at 1168. [At 227 some women are in jail but at
444-48 they are miraculously let loose and return to the mountain.]

39: 'roofless rocks': The unusual turn of phrase highlights the wildness of Mt.
Cithaeron. This mountain world of Dionysiac worship represents the antithesis of Pentheus' walled city of Thebes.

40: The theme of learning (*manthanein*) is frequent (39, 657, 1113, 1281, 1296, 1345;
cp. 480, 490). Dionysus *will* teach the whole city (cp. 48, 1295) of his divinity
whether they want to learn it or not.

40: The main reason Dionysus has come to Thebes is to establish his mysteries (cp.
22, 49, 465, 1387).

45: **'A fighter against the gods':** The important word *theo-machos* appears three
times in the *Bacchae* and nowhere else in Greek tragedy. Resisting the gods
always ends disastrously. See Glossary, 'God-fighter.'

from his libations and mentions me nowhere in his prayers.°
For this reason I shall show him and all Thebans
that I am a god. After setting matters here in order
I will move on to another land, revealing myself there too.
But if the city of Thebans,° with wrath and weapons, 50
seeks to drive the Bacchae down from the mountain
I will wage war on the city,° marshalling my army of maenads.°
For this reason I have changed my appearance to a mortal one
and transformed my shape into the nature of a man.°

*[Dionysus turns and addresses the entering chorus; they show no sign of
hearing him]*
Hail, my sisterhood of worshippers,° you who left Mt. Tmolus,° 55
bulwark of Lydia, women I wooed from foreign lands.
Comrades in rest, companions of the road,
raise up those drums° native to Phrygia's cities,
the invention of mother Rhea° and myself.
Surround this royal house of Pentheus! 60
Strike your drums so that Cadmus' city may come to see!

46: **Pentheus the atheist?** The chorus calls him 'godless' at 995 (= 1015) but that is
not the case. He does not consider Dionysus a god (220, 242-47, 333, 517), so
he refuses to worship him (cp. Dodds 95; Kirk 99).
50: 'If the city...' Note that Dionysus does not *unconditionally* predict the play's outcome: "While it is certain that Dionysus will be accepted at Thebes in the
end, the strength and manner of the opposition remains unknown, and much
of the suspense of the next 750 lines derives from this." (Taplin 56)
52: **Dionysus as a military leader:** Euripides sets up his audience by having the
Stranger *suggest* that the climax might involve a blood-bath between Thebes
and Dionysus (cp. 784, 809, 845). That may have been the traditional legend
but the dramatist will surprise us with something much more horrific. [For
Dionysus as *general* of the Bacchae see Aeschylus' *Eumenides* 25-26 (458 B.C.).]
52: **Maenads** ('frenzied women') are the same as Bacchae ('female devotees of
Bacchus'), though the term *maenads* (occurring mainly in the play's second
half) highlights their frenzy. See Glossary, 'Maenads.'
54: **Dionysus' human disguise and its motive:** He does not want to force Pentheus,
as he had forced the Theban women, to recognize his divinity. It will mean
much more if Pentheus, by his own volition, recognizes the unexpected divine guest; hence the repeated emphasis on human disguise (3, 53-54).
55: **'Sisterhood of worshippers':** *Thiasos* is the religious term for cult groups de-
voted to Dionysus. Being under the god's control, they act in unison toward
a specific goal. See Glossary, 'Thiasos.'
55: Tmolus: Mountain in Asia Minor, sacred (64) to Dionysus. See Glossary, 'Mountains.'
58: **'Drums':** The play's main musical instrument, carried throughout by the Asian
chorus. It was a small wooden hoop resembling a tambourine but covered
on *both* sides with hide. See Glossary, 'Drum.'
59: Rhea: A Greek goddess (a Titan, sister and wife of Kronos, and mother of Zeus)
who is here identified with the Asiatic goddess Cybele, the great Mother
Goddess of Phrygia in Asia Minor (see 79n.).

Meanwhile I shall hasten to the folds of Mt. Cithaeron
to join the choral dances of my Theban Bacchae.

*[Exit Dionysus, stage left, towards Cithaeron; enter Chorus, orchestra left,
wearing dresses, fawnskins and (probably) turbans. Each bacchant carries a
tambourine-like drum.]*

Choral Entrance Song°

Prelude

From the land of Asia I hasten, leaving behind Tmolus, sacred mountain,
swift in my sweet toiling for Bromios the Roaring God°   65
wearied but not wearied,
praising Bacchus, crying out "euoi."°
Who is in the street, in the street?°
Who is in the palace? Let him come outside to watch.
Let everyone keep their lips pure in holy silence.° I shall forever sing 70
in Dionysus' honor the hymns that custom has prescribed.

Hymn to Dionysus°

Strophe 1

O blessed is he who, happy in his heart,°

FIRST CHORAL SONG (64-169): The chorus of fifteen Asiatic Bacchae now enters
the orchestra. The young, vigorous women, in their maenadic costumes and
masks, sing and dance excitedly to the music of a reed-piper. Their complex
cultic hymn is composed of three parts: the *prelude* (64-71), sung during entry; the *hymn* itself (72-134), composed of four stanzas (two strophes or 'turns'
and two anti-strophes or 'counter-turns'); and the *epode* or conclusion (135-
69) whose unusual length constitutes virtually another hymn. The song's function is to present "the orgiastic cult to the audience in clear outlines as the
norm, as the back-cloth against which the events of the plot will be played
out." (Oranje 157). See also Glossary, 'Chorus.'

65: **Bromios** ('the Roarer'): A cult name of Dionysus (22x in the *Bacchae*). See Glossary, 'Bromios.'

67: 'Euoi': An exclamation of joy used in the cult of Dionysus to praise the god (cp. 129,
140, 151, 158). Hence the god himself is sometimes called "Euios" (cp. 566, 579).

68: "Who is in the street, in the street?" is one of this song's three cultic formulas
(cp. 83, 152; 116, 165).

70: Reverential silence customarily preceded ritual acts such as this 'cultic' entrance
by the chorus.

72-134: Hymns to Dionysus are very rare in tragedy. The only other extant one is
the sixth and final choral ode (1115-54) of Sophocles' *Antigone* (c. 442 B.C.).

72: **a)** 'O blessed (*makar*) is he': the formulaic language of the traditional *makar-
ismos*, i.e. the praise of the blessed status of those who have *seen* the mysteries;
cp. 902-11. **b)** Why is the bacchant described as male? Given that there seem to
have been few male adherents to Dionysus' rites (though cp. 114), the masculine pronoun here probably represents a generalizing usage; as the context indicates the chorus is thinking of female worshippers (Kirk 82). **c)** 'happy in his
heart' (*eudaimôn*): One of the play's most important words, occurring more
often (nine times) than in any other Greek tragedy. *Eudaimonia* consists of being in right relationship to a divine power. See Glossary, 'Happiness.'

knows the initiation rites of the gods,°
purifies his life and
joins his soul to the cult group,°   75
dancing on the mountains, with holy purifications°
celebrating the Bacchic rituals.
O blessed the man who dutifully observes
the mysteries of the Great Mother, Cybele.°
Swinging high the thyrsus   80
and crowned in ivy°
he serves Dionysus.
Onward you Bacchae, onward Bacchae, °
escort the roaring Bromios home,
a god and the son of a god! Escort him   85
down from the Phrygian mountains into Greece's wide-wayed
streets, streets wide for dancing, Bromios the Roaring God!

Antistrophe 1°
At that time when Dionysus' mother was pregnant
Zeus' thunder flew down
forcing her into the pangs of labor.   90
She thrust the child from her womb prematurely

73: Knowledge of the Dionysiac mysteries was secret. See Glossary, 'Mysteries, Dionysiac.'

75: **Joining one's soul** (*psyche*) **to the cult group** (*thiasos*)**:** The usual understanding of this famous line is that it refers to the soul's union with god or to a loss of the self as a result of the merging of individual with group consciousness as physical exhaustion is translated into physical well-being (Dodds 76; Henrichs 1982, 224). For an alternative explanation see Glossary, 'Thiasos.'

76: 'Holy purifications': Precise interpretation is uncertain; perhaps it refers to some preliminary physical purification that would ritually cleanse the worshipper or to the psychic release brought about by participating in the mountain dancing of the *thiasos*.

72-77: **Prerequisites for Dionysiac happiness:** a) knowledge of the mysteries; b) living a pure life; c) initiation into the *thiasos*; d) participation in the mountain rituals honoring Dionysus. Note that the Dionysiac mysteries of the *Bacchae* emphasize happiness *in the here and now of this world* rather than in the next world like the Eleusinian mysteries (Dodds 75; Oranje 111); but for happiness in the afterlife, see Glossary, 'Mysteries, Dionysiac.'

79: Cybele: An Asiatic goddess worshipped in Asia Minor as the 'Great Mother' of all living things. Her worship spread to Greece where her foreign elements were tamed by being identified with Demeter (in cult) and Rhea (in myth).

81: **Ivy as a symbol**: Dionysus' worshippers were, like their thyrsi, crowned with ivy (106, 177, 313, 341, 531, 703). Being 'ever-green' ivy symbolized the vine god's vigor and vitality. See Glossary, 'Ivy.'

83: Another ritual cry, like "Who is in the street?" (68); it recurs at 152-53.

First antistrophe (88-104): There are three myths here: a) 88-93: Dionysus' premature thunder-birth from Semele; b) 94-100: Dionysus' supernatural second birth from Zeus' thigh; c) 101-4: the myth explaining why the Maenads crown themselves with garlands of snakes.

and was herself slain by the bolt of lightning.
Immediately Zeus, the son of Cronus,
received the baby in his own birth chambers
concealing it in his thigh.   95
Stitching his leg back together
with golden clasps
he hid the infant from Hera.°
When the Fates ordained it°
Zeus gave birth to a bull-horned god°   100
and crowned him with crowns of snakes.
This is why maenads fling round in their hair
beast-eating snakes, the spoil of their hunting.

Strophe 2
O Thebes, nurse of Semele,   105
crown yourself with ivy!°
Abound, abound
with rich berry-laden evergreen creepers!
Rave with bacchic frenzy
carrying your branches of oak or fir!   110
Crown your garments of dappled deerskin°
with the fleece of white wool!
Make the violent fennel-wands holy all round!°
Immediately the whole land will dance

88-98: **Zeus' two male pregnancies:** Besides giving birth to Dionysus from his thigh,
Zeus gave birth to Athena from his head (after swallowing his first wife, the
pregnant Metis; Hesiod *Theogony* 899, 924). Depictions on vase paintings of
Dionysus' birth are not often found; in contrast, paintings of Athena's birth
are frequent. Compare Yahweh's making of Eve from Adam's rib (*Genesis* 2.
21-23).

99: The Fates: The three spinning sisters who regulated each individual's life.

100: Zeus' pregnancy completes its term whereas Semele's is premature (91) (Dodds
79).

106: By crowning itself with ivy Thebes would become a convert to Dionysiac worship.

111: **Deerskin and its significance:** This traditional cloak of the maenads was sacred
(137) for several reasons: it protected them during their cold winter rituals on
the mountain; it brought them into communion with the world of nature; it
helped them to assume a new identity, namely that of a wild animal whose
bounding swiftness and freedom of movement (cp. 862-76) were virtues that
would naturally be attractive to these spirited devotees of Dionysus.

113: **Potential violence of the thyrsus:** Of this paradoxical sentence Dodds (82)
writes: "The startling conjunction of *holiness* and *violence* (*hybris*) expresses
the dual aspect of Dionysiac ritual as an act of controlled violence in which
dangerous natural forces are subdued to a religious purpose. The thyrsus is
the vehicle of these forces; its touch can work beneficent miracles (704 ff.),
but can also inflict injury (762)...." [Another possible translation of 113: "Make
yourselves holy by handling the violent wands."]

whenever the roaring Bromios leads the bands of revellers   115
to the mountain, to the mountain °
where the female mob waits
driven away from their looms and shuttles°
stung by the goad of Dionysus.

Antistrophe 2°
O secret chamber of the Kouretes°   120
and holy haunts of Crete,
haunts where Zeus was born,
where in their caves the triple-crested Korybantes
invented for me this cylinder
covered with tightly stretched hide.   125
During the intense bacchic dancing they mixed its sound
with the sweet-humming breath of Phrygian reed-pipes
putting the drum into Mother Rhea's hands
to beat out time for the joyous cries of the Bacchae.
From the divine Mother the frenzied Satyrs°   130
won the instrument for themselves
and joined it to the dances
of the biennial festivals
in which Dionysus delights.°

Epode°
Sweet is the pleasure the god brings us in the mountains   135

116: **Mountain as *the* place for the activity of the Maenads:** '*To the mountain, to the
    mountain*' is another cultic formula (cp. 68, 83); it recurs at 165, 977, 987. This
    formula "must have been used in real cult as a maenadic signal which opened
    the *oreibasia* (mountain dancing of the maenads)." (Henrichs 1978, 149). Cp.
    135-39n.
118: Looms and shuttles: These instruments of weaving are symbolic of the female's
    loyalty to her home and husband (cp. 1236-37; also Penelope's great woven
    shroud for Odysseus' father, Laertes, at *Odyssey* 24. 128-48).
Second antistrophe (120-34): Relates the myth of the origin of the (tambourine-
    like) drum: a) 120-25: its invention in Crete by the Kouretes to save baby
    Zeus; b) 126-29: its presentation to Rhea, Zeus' mother, to use in her sacred
    rites; c) 130-34: its presentation to the satyrs to use in the rites of Dionysus.
        The Satyrs, as male devotees, stand in the same relation to Dionysus as the
    Kouretes do to Rhea Cybele.
120: Kouretes (= Korybantes): The male devotees of Rhea Cybele (mother of the
    Zeus-child). As their name indicates they were guardians of the *kouros* ('youth')
    or infant Zeus.
130: Satyrs: Immortal fertility spirits of the wild who were hybrids of man and beast.
134: Every other year at Delphi, in the uplands of Mt. Parnassus, a night festival in
    mid-winter was held in which women danced under torch-light in honor of
    Dionysus (cp. Sophocles' *Antigone* 1126-30).
135-69: **Conclusion of first choral ode:** Sung to a complex and rapidly changing
    blend of expressive meters, the conclusion (or epode) forms a powerful emo-
    tional climax to the chorus' hymn. The interpretation of these lines has long

when from the running revellers
he falls to the ground clad in his sacred fawnskin. Hunting
the blood of slaughtered goats for the joy of devouring raw flesh
he rushes through the mountains of Lydia, of Phrygia.°
Hail to the Roaring God, Bromios our leader! Euoi!   140
The ground flows with milk,
flows with wine,
flows with the nectar of bees.°
The Bacchic One,° lifting high
the bright-burning flame of the pine-torch,   145
like the smoke of Syrian frankincense,
springs up and rushes along with his wand of fennel.
Running and dancing he incites any wanderers,
shakes them with shouts of joy
tossing his luxuriant locks to the wind.   150
Amidst the cries of "euoi" he roars out:
   "Onward you Bacchae,
   Onward Bacchae,
   glittering pride of gold-flowing Mt. Tmolus.°
   Sing and dance for Dionysus   155
   as the rumbling drums roar!
   Glorify him joyously!
   "Euoi, euoi!" Yes, sing out
   your Phrygian incantations.

---

been vexed. The thematic structure seems to be as follows: a) 135-43: description of Dionysus as ritual leader and miracle-worker; b) 144-51: description of the dancing god as he inspires his worshippers; c) 152-65: the god's actual exhortation to his devotees.

135-39: **The three key elements of Dionysiac ritual:** a) going to the mountain to dance (*orei-basia*), which took place only in the winter; b) tearing-to-pieces an animal's body (*sparagmos*); c) devouring the animal's raw flesh (*omo-phagia*). Note that the hunting, killing and eating of animals is done here only by Dionysus, not the maenads; hence he is sometimes described as 'Raw-Eater.' See Glossary, 'Tearing-to-pieces.'

143: This first mention of Dionysus' miracles foreshadows precisely the maenads' miracle at 699-713.

144: **Who is 'the Bacchic One'?** Dionysus himself and *not*, as most scholars (e.g. Dodds) have thought until recently, the god temporarily incarnate in a male celebrant or priest who acts as the maenads' ritual leader (Henrichs 1984, 73-85). Although Dionysus desires honor from male and female alike (206-9) and although Tiresias and Cadmus will speak of going to Mt. Cithaeron in their maenadic costumes to dance in honor of the god (183-95), the play nowhere presents men as possessed by Dionysus nor are they celebrants in his ecstatic worship; the one exception is Pentheus but he will be a victim not a celebrant.

154: 'Gold-flowing Mt. Tmolus' refers to the gold dust carried down Tmolus (cp. 13, 55) and into the Pactolus, a tributary of the Hermus River in central Asia Minor.

As the holy flute   160
roars holy hymns,
glorify him, maenads,
as you climb
to the mountain,
to the mountain!"   165
Sweetly rejoicing, then,
like a filly grazing with her mother,
the bacchant leaps
swift and nimble on her feet.°

ACT I°

[Enter Tiresias slowly and without escort, stage right; he wears a white mask
and is dressed like a bacchant, carrying a thyrsus and sporting a fawnskin
cloak.]

Tiresias [knocking at the palace door]
Who is at the gates? Call Cadmus from the palace,   170
Agenor's son, who, after leaving the city of Sidon,°
fenced this citadel of Thebes with ramparts.
[The door opens and a servant appears]
Let someone go and announce that Tiresias is looking for him.
He knows why I have come and what arrangements I have made. 175
Though I'm an old man and he still older, we will twine together
    thyrsi
and wear fawnskin cloaks and crown our heads with shoots of ivy.

[Enter Cadmus from the palace, also dressed like a bacchant.]

Cadmus
O dearest friend, how delighted I was to hear the wise voice
of a wise man when I was in the palace.
I have come prepared, wearing these trappings of the god.   180

168-69: Leaping bacchantes: Dionysiac dance involved "a swinging of the head, the
    shoulders, and the upper part of the body, first to one side and then to the
    other, as the dancer advances." (Leinieks 61)
ACT I (170-369): Thebes' two most prominent authorities, the old 'believers' Tire-
    sias and Cadmus (city seer and city founder), encounter the young sceptic
    Pentheus (king). This preliminary confrontation is necessary because "before
    we see Dionysus and Pentheus in collision we must be introduced to each of
    them separately, so that we may understand the strength and obstinacy of the
    colliding forces" (Dodds 90). In short, Act I sets the stage for the main event,
    the fierce power struggle of Acts II, III, and IV (434-976). Note that the two
    outer scenes (170-214 = 45 lines, 330-369 = 40 lines) frame the longer center
    episode (215-329 = 115 lines) which features the contest between the young
    prince and Apollo's blind old prophet.
171: Sidon: A major port city of Phoenicia (modern Syria) ruled by Agenor.

As vigorously as we can we must exalt Dionysus to greatness
since he is my daughter's son [who has revealed himself as a god
   among men.]°
Where must we go to dance?
Where ply our feet?
Where shake our grey heads?   185
Old man to old man, instruct me, Tiresias. You're the expert.
I won't tire, day or night,
striking the ground with my thyrsus.
Gladly we've forgotten that we're old men.

Tiresias
                  Then you experience the same excitement I do.°
For I, too, feel young and will try to dance.°   190

Cadmus
Then shall we not take a chariot to the mountain?°

Tiresias
But if we don't go on foot, the god wouldn't be honored in the same
   way.

Cadmus
Shall I lead you, one old man guiding another, like a tutor does a
   child?

Tiresias
The god will lead us there without toil.°

Cadmus
And will we be the only men in the city to dance in honor
   of Bacchus?   195

182: Brackets here and throughout usually indicate that the enclosed text is prob-
    ably spurious.
189: The play's first example of *antilabe*, i.e. division of a single line between speak-
    ers. "It usually suggests excitement - here perhaps Tiresias' excited pleasure
    in comparing symptoms." (Dodds 93). *Antilabe* is rare in *Bacchae*; the most
    important instance is 966-70. See Glossary, 'Stichomythia.'
189-214: **Opening dialogue of Tiresias and Cadmus.** The point here is "to exhibit a
    Dionysiac miracle of rejuvenation: by the magic of the god they are filled for
    a time with 'a mysterious strength and exaltation'.... If the old men are filled
    with power, it should be because they are filled with faith. But Cadmus at
    least is not filled with faith, only with a timid worldliness. His real creed is
    'the solidarity of the family.' "(Dodds 90) Although the two men, whose old
    age is repeatedly emphasized (185-207), speak of dancing (183, 205) there is
    no explicit indication that they do (cp. 1224).
191-99: The play's first example of *stichomythia*, i. e. alternating *single* line dialogue,
    a common convention of tragedy used at moments of excitement and con-
    frontation. See Glossary, 'Stichomythia.'
194: This kind of Dionysiac effortlessness is a frequent motif (cp. 66, 614, 1128).

Tiresias
Yes, since only we reason well. The rest are fools!°

Cadmus *[finally yielding]*
We're tarrying too long. Come on, take hold of my hand.

Tiresias *[stretching out his hand]*
Here, then. Let's join hands so we make a pair.

Cadmus
Since I'm a mortal, I'll not despise the gods.

Tiresias *[taking Cadmus' hand]*
We don't use clever subtleties on the gods.   200
For there is no argument that throws down the ancestral traditions,°
those we received from our fathers, possessions as old as time itself.
No, not even the cleverness schemed up by the sharpest minds!

Cadmus
Will someone say that I show no respect for old age
just because I intend to dance all decked out in ivy wreaths?   205

Tiresias
No! For the god has not determined whether it is the young
or the old who must dance. On the contrary,
he wishes to receive honors in common from everyone
counting nobody out in his desire to be exalted.

[Enter Pentheus, stage left, in a hurry; he is dressed in his royal robes and attended by guards.] °

Cadmus
Since you can't see this light of day, Tiresias,   210
my words will proclaim for you what is going on.
Here comes Pentheus, Echion's son, running towards the house.
It is to him that I have entrusted the power of this land.
How flustered he is! What calamity, I wonder, will he report?

Pentheus° *[at first not noticing Cadmus and Tiresias]*
While I happened to be out of the country   215

196: The implication is that the rest of Thebes' men believed, like Pentheus, that Bacchus was a sham.

201: 'Throwing down the ancestral traditions': this wrestling metaphor alludes to a type of fifth-century agnosticism made famous by the sophist Protagoras who began one of his *Throwing-down (= Destructive) Essays* as follows: "Concerning the gods I cannot know whether they exist or do not exist or what form they have." (cp. Dodds 94-95) See Glossary, 'Sophist.'

215: **Pentheus' age:** About 18-20 years; he is 'a young man' at 274, 974; see Glossary, 'Pentheus' age.'

215-62: **Pentheus' monologue as a second prologue,** "a counter-manifesto to the first (prologue) - having heard the god's programme of action, we now listen to man's." (Dodds 97)

I heard about strange new evils throughout the city —
that our women have abandoned their homes
for the sham revelries of Bacchus
frisking about on the dark-shadowed mountains
honoring with their dances the latest god, Dionysus, whoever he is. 220
They've set up their mixing bowls brimming with wine
amidst their cult gatherings and each lady slinks off in a different direction
to some secluded wilderness to service the lusts of men.°
They pretend to be maenads performing sacrifices
but in reality they rank Aphrodite's pleasures before Bacchus! 225
     I've shackled with chains all those I captured
and thrown them into the public jails where my soldiers keep guard.
And all those who remain at large, I'll hunt down from the mountains°
[Ino and Agave, who bore me to Echion,
and Actaeon's mother, I mean Autonoe.]° 230
After fastening them tight in nets of iron
I'll put a stop quickly to their destructive bacchic revelry.
     They say, too, that some stranger has come here
a quack dealer in spells from the land of Lydia
his long locks and golden curls all sweet-smelling 235
his cheeks dark as wine, his eyes full of Aphrodite's charms.
Day and night he surrounds himself with young girls
alluring them with his mysteries of joy.
But if I capture him within this land
I'll put a stop to his beating the thyrsus and tossing his hair. 240
In fact I'll cut his head right off his body!°
     This is the guy who claims that Dionysus is a *god*.
Indeed he claims that Dionysus was once sewn into Zeus' thigh.
The truth is that Dionysus was incinerated by fiery lightning
along with his mother Semele because she had lied about her union
with Zeus.° Aren't these terrible slanders worthy of hanging? 246
What outrageous acts of hybris this stranger commits, whoever he is!°

222-23: **Pentheus' sexual perversity?** Dodds (97) uses this passage and others like it
    to justify his neo-Freudian characterization of Pentheus as "the dark puritan
    whose passion is compounded of horror and unconscious desire." That seems
    too strong. See Glossary, 'Pentheus as Peeping Tom.'

228: **Pentheus as a hunter:** The image is frequent (e.g. 839, 871, 960, 1022).

229-30: [Lines probably interpolated]; Semele's sisters reappear at 681-82, 1091,
    1124-30, 1227-30.

241: There is a gruesome irony in Pentheus' imagining that he will decapitate
    Dionysus (cp. 1139-43).

244-46: "The truth is...": This is an abbreviated version of the 'truth' that Pentheus'
    aunts believed; see 26-31. Like them, he will be punished for not believing in
    the divinity of Dionysus.

246-47: These lines conclude the main section of Pentheus' opening speech (215-62).
    His talk of hanging the Stranger and the powerful expression *hybreis hybrizein*

[Pentheus, as he turns to enter the palace, finally notices Cadmus and Tiresias]
But here's another wonder. I see the sign-reader,
Tiresias, outfitted in dappled fawnskins
and my own mother's father. How completely laughable,°   250
revelling about with his thyrsus like a bacchant!
I am ashamed, sir,° to see your old age so devoid of common sense.
Won't you shake off that ivy!
Won't you get your hands free of that thyrsus, grandfather?

[Turning abruptly from Cadmus to Tiresias]
It's you, Tiresias, who have persuaded him to this folly.   255
By introducing yet another new divinity to mankind, you hope
for more augury from the birds and more money from reading the omens
in the sacrificial fires.° If hoary old age weren't protecting you
you'd be sitting in chains with the rest of the Bacchae
for importing these sinister rituals. For whenever the liquid joy   260
of the grape comes into women's festivals, then, I assure you,°
there's nothing wholesome in their rites.

Chorus-Leader
What impiety! Don't you respect the gods, stranger?
Don't you respect Cadmus who sowed the earth-born crop?°
Are you, the son of Echion, going to shame his race?°   265

Tiresias° *[letting go of Cadmus' hand]*
Whenever a wise man sets out to argue an honest case

'to commit hybristic acts of hybris' (247; cp. 1297) reveal the ferocity of his
    opposition to the new Bacchic cult and its leader. See Glossary, 'Hybris.'
250: **Laughter (mockery) as a weapon of ridicule in a 'shame culture':** Pentheus
    is unusual in that he dispenses scorn whereas most tragic characters fear it.
    See Glossary, 'Laughter.'
252: Pentheus rebukes his grandfather sharply but respectfully; that respect doesn't
    extend to Tiresias.
257: That money is what motivated prophets was a common charge (e. g. *Antigone*
    1055, *Oed. Rex* 388).
260-61: Pentheus implies that the maenads intoxicate themselves with wine. As we
    soon learn from the first messenger (686-88), this insinuation is not true; the
    maenads preferred water and milk (704-10).
264: **Cadmus and the myth of the Sown Men:** Cadmus slew the dragon guarding
    Thebes and sowed its teeth, from which, miraculously, sprang earth-born
    warriors ('the sown men') with whose help he founded the city. See Glos-
    sary, 'Cadmus.'
265: **Shame:** On the importance of shame (vs. guilt) in Greek society see Glossary,
    'Shame culture.'
266-327: **Tiresias' refutation of Pentheus:** The prophet's upshot is well put by
    Rijksbaron (165-66): "The attention Teiresias pays to Pentheus' concern, the
    Theban women, is negligible when compared with that paid to Dionysos....
    The message is clear: rather than occupying himself with the Theban women

it's no great undertaking to argue well.
Your tongue runs smooth like a wheel, as if you were a man of reason,
but your words reveal no reason.
If he behaves recklessly, an able and articulate man   270
turns out to be a bad citizen because he lacks good sense.°
Now as for this new god whom your laughter mocks
I couldn't describe his greatness and how powerful he'll be
throughout Greece. For there are two things, young man,
that are the primary elements among humans. First there's the goddess Demeter.   275
She's the earth but you can call her by whatever name you wish.°
She nourishes mortals with dry foods. But he who came afterward,
Semele's offspring, discovered the wet drink of the grape
as a counter-balance to Demeter's bread. He introduced it
to mortals to stop their sorrow and pain.°   280
Whenever men are filled with the stream of the grape-vine
they can sleep and forget the evils of the day.
No other medicine alleviates human suffering.
Dionysus, being a god, is poured out as a libation to the gods
so that it is through him that men receive blessings.   285
    Furthermore, why do you laugh at him and the story
that he was sewn into Zeus' thigh? I'll teach you how elegant this is.
When Zeus snatched the infant from the fiery thunderbolt and carried him
up to Mt. Olympus as a god, Hera wanted to throw the child out of
    heaven.
But Zeus contrived a counter-scheme such as only a god could devise.
Breaking off a part of the sky that encircles the earth he fashioned one
    piece   291
into a dummy Dionysus. Using this as an offering of *peace*
Zeus palmed off the dummy as the real thing to Hera, thus pacifying
her hostility.° Over time humans, changing the word *sky*,

---

and with Teiresias and Kadmos, Pentheus should be concerned about his
own behaviour...considering the importance of the new god."
270-71: The danger of 'word merchants': "Reflections on the harm done by the art
    of suggestion (*peithô*), when it is exercised by men without principle, appear
    repeatedly in Euripides, and seem to represent a lesson he wished to bring
    home to his audience.... This in fact was the greatest danger of ancient as of
    modern democracies."(Dodds 103) See Glossary, 'Sophist.'
276: Demeter as Earth Goddess: Tiresias is referring here to the fact that many Greeks
    derived the name 'De-meter' from *gê mêtêr* which means 'earth mother.'
279-80: **Dionysus as the inventor of wine:** Bread and wine, the two staples of the an-
    cient Mediterranean diet, were the gifts of Demeter and Dionysus respectively;
    in practice, however, wine was rarely drunk by women. (Henrichs 1982, 140)
294: Tiresias does not say what Zeus did with the real Dionysus but the *Homeric
    Hymn to Dionysus* (26. 3-5) says that Hermes, the messenger god and son of
    Zeus, brought him to the nymphs on Mt. Nysa. Tiresias appears as a kind of

have come to say that he was sown in Zeus' *thigh*.   295
This story was invented because people couldn't
believe that Dionysus, a god, had once been held hostage to Hera, a
   goddess.
This god is a mantic prophet too. For Bacchic revelry
and mania produce much mantic power:°
whenever this god comes into the body in full force°   300
he makes the frenzied foretell the future.°
He also shares some of Ares' bellicose spirit;°
for fear sends panic through a marching militia
dispersing the battle formation before it ever even touches the spear:
This, too, comes from Dionysus.°   305
One day you will even see him on the cliffs of Delphi
bounding with pine torches across the plateau between Parnassus'
   twin peaks
brandishing and shaking his Bacchic wand.°
He shall be made mighty throughout Greece. So obey me, Pentheus.
Don't be so sure that force is what dominates human affairs.   310
nor if you have an opinion but that opinion is sick, imagine that your
   opinion

'theological sophist.' His string of puns here ('piece...peace, sky...thigh') is
the most remarkable etymological argument in the 350 year span of archaic
and classical Greek literature (Stanford 175). The blind seer uses word-play
to spearhead his attack on Pentheus' refusal to believe the myth of Dionysus'
double birth. Despite Tiresias' claim (200) that he is not using cleverness
(*sophia*) on the gods, he does present himself as the worst sort of sophist,
combining a certain religious conservatism with a flare for relativism that
was so popular in the late fifth century. See Glossary, 'Sophist.'
299: Tiresias again makes an etymological connection, this time between 'madness'
   (*mania*) and 'mantic' (*mantis*,'seer'; cp. our 'praying mantis'). The mantic 'sees'
   because he is driven mad by some higher power.
300: The god inside the body of his prophet? It is hard to know whether Tiresias
   means that the god himself actually occupies the human subject (so Dodds
   109) or whether he is equating the god with wine, as at 284 (so the ancient
   biographer Plutarch *Moralia* 432e; cp. Leinieks 95-97).
298-301: These lines about Dionysus' mantic power anticipate his prophecy at the
   play's end (1330-39).
302-5: These lines about Dionysus' power to make an army panic (an attribute
   usually assigned to Pan) foreshadow the Theban Bacchae sending Pentheus'
   soldiers into flight on the mountain (761-64).
298-305: The frenzy of prophecy and fear: "The attribution of the functions of Apollo
   and Ares to Dionysus is the result of Teiresias' desire to magnify the god as
   much as possible in his argument with Pentheus.... The connection is that all
   three gods affect their human subjects with frenzy." (Leinieks 80)
308: Delphi as Dionysus' domain? Usually we think of Delphi as the sanctuary of
   Apollo and his oracle. But Tiresias' prediction here about Dionysus' acceptance
   at Delphi corresponds to the historical facts.

makes you somehow wise. Accept the god into this land and pour
libations to him!
Become a bacchant and crown your head with a wreath!
   It is not Dionysus who will force women to be self-controlled
in Aphrodite's realm. No, their chastity resides in their nature.° 315
[Self-control in all things always depends on character.]°
Just consider the facts. For even in the revelries of Bacchus
the self-controlled woman, at least, will not be corrupted.°
   You see how you rejoice whenever the crowds gather
at the palace gates and the city glorifies the name of Pentheus. 320
Dionysus too, I am sure, takes delight in receiving honor.
So I, for one, and Cadmus, whom your laughter mocks,
both of us will crown ourselves with ivy and dance,
a grey-haired old pair. But still we must dance.
Nor will I fight against the gods because I've been pressured° 325
by your words. For you are most painfully mad so that
neither with drugs nor without them could you cure your disease.°

Chorus-Leader
Old man, you do not shame Apollo by your words.
Indeed, by honoring the great god Bromios, you reveal your wisdom.

Cadmus
My son, Tiresias has advised you well. 330
Live with us rather than outside the law.
For now you flutter about and think without thinking well.
Even if this god does not exist, as you claim,
let him be considered a god in your eyes. Lie for a good cause,
say that he is Semele's child. In this way she might seem 335

315: **What determines human ethics?** "It is *physis* [personal character], not *nomos*
[social convention] that determines conduct.... Here once more Teiresias
speaks the language of the fifth century and thinks in terms popularized by
the Sophistic movement." (Dodds 111). See Glossary, 'Sophist.'
316: Brackets (here and throughout) indicate, unless otherwise noted, that the lines
are probably spurious.
314-18: **Dionysus as beyond good and evil?** Tiresias is responding to Pentheus'
charge (at 222-25) of the maenads' sexual immorality. As Dodds (111) observes,
"Dionysus is not immoral; he is non-moral—morality is irrelevant to religion
of the Dionysiac type...."
325: 'Fighting against the gods': in refusing to do this Tiresias is the opposite of
Pentheus (cp. 45).
326-27: The prophet's riddle: Is Tiresias referring to real drugs added to the wine
of the initiate in Dionysiac cult or to the medicating wisdom of his own
words (Leinieks 116)? Whichever is the case, Tiresias seems to be implicitly
contrasting his own healthy and *natural* frenzy, inspired by Dionysus (305),
with Pentheus' unhealthy and *artificial* frenzy (in fighting against the god).

to have given birth to a god and honor might accrue to our entire family.°
You see the horrific death of Actaeon,
how the dogs he bred ripped him to pieces
and ate his raw flesh after he boasted in the mountain meadows
that he was better than Artemis at hunting with hounds.°   340
Don't let that happen to you.
[holding an ivy wreath out for Pentheus]
     Come here. Let me crown you with ivy.
Join us in giving honor to the god.

Pentheus *[pulling back quickly]*
Get your hand away from me! Go play the revelling bacchant
but don't wipe that folly of yours off on me!
I'm going to punish this teacher of your mindlessness.   345

[Turning to his attendants]
Guard, off quickly!
Go to the seat where this seer here reads his birds.
Tear it up with crowbars.
Turn the whole place upside down!°
Toss his sacred woolen wreaths to the blowing winds.   350
Then he'll really feel my sting!

[Exit a guard down one of the side-ramps]
     And you other guards, go up through the city
and track down this effeminate looking stranger°
who brings a new disease to the women and dishonors their beds.
And if you capture him, lead him here in chains   355
so that he's brought to justice by being stoned to death°
and sees a bitter bacchic revelry in Thebes!

[Exit other guards down the other side-ramp]

Tiresias
O wretched man, how ignorant you are of what you're saying!

336: The important issue for Cadmus and Tiresias is not *why* they accept Dionysus
but simply *that* they accept him. It is family pride, not truth, that motivates
Cadmus, thus calling to mind Plato's observation: "There are many who carry
the thyrsus but few who are devotees of Bacchus." (*Phaedo* 69c)

337-40: **Actaeon as a negative role model:** Pentheus' cousin was the paradigm of
the hunted hunter. See Glossary, 'Actaeon.'

349: Tiresias' bird observatory actually existed at Thebes (as did Semele's memorial
tomb mentioned in lines 6-9). It was one of the 'sights' on the tourist circuit
according to the travel writer Pausanias (second century A.D.) who reports in
his *Guide to Greece* (9.16.1) that it was behind the temple of Zeus Ammon.

353: **Dionysus' effeminacy:** on its origin and significance see Glossary, 'Dionysus,
androgyny.'

356: First Pentheus threatened decapitation (240-41), then hanging (246), now ston-
ing (356-57).

Now you're completely mad whereas before you had only momen-
tarily lost your mind.
    Let's go, Cadmus, and on behalf of this man,   360
even though he is savage, and on behalf of the city,
let us beseech the god to do nothing sinister.
Come with me and bring your ivy staff.
You try to support my body and I'll try to support yours.
It is a shameful thing for two old men to fall.   365
Still, let come what may, since we must be slaves to Bacchus, Zeus'
    son.°
But beware, Cadmus, lest Pentheus bring the pain pent up in his
    name°
into your house. I don't say this by any prophetic skill but rather
on account of the facts. For Pentheus is a fool and says foolish things.°
[*Exit Cadmus and Tiresias, stage left, propping one another, using their
thyrsi as canes, heading off to Mt. Cithaeron; Pentheus stays on stage*]

Chorus of Asian Bacchae°
Strophe 1
    O Holiness, queen of the gods!°   370
    O Holiness, as you make your way
    on golden wings across the earth,
    do you hear these words of Pentheus?
    Do you hear his hybris,
    blaspheming Bromios, Semele's son,   375
    he who is first among the blessed divinities
    at the banquets decked with bright bouquets?
    For Dionysus has the power

366: Indenture to Dionysus: In *Oedipus the King* Tiresias considers himself a slave
    to Apollo (410); here he considers himself (and Cadmus) a slave to Dionysus.
    Pentheus would never stoop to such 'grovelling.'
367: **Meaning of Pentheus' name:** *Pentheus* as bringer of *penthos*, 'pain'. This is
    Tiresias' third and most charged pun on Pentheus' name as 'Man of Pain.'
    See Glossary, 'Pentheus' name.'
215-369: **Note the order of speakers in this three actor scene** (a-b-c-a-b): Pentheus
    (215-62), Tiresias (266-327), Cadmus (330-42) Pentheus (343-57), Tiresias (358-
    69). In Euripidean debates the 'winning' speaker usually comes second; so
    here Tiresias, in each case, follows Pentheus.
369: Tiresias' acting role is now over; he will not appear again. Cadmus reappears
    at the end (1216 ff.).
SECOND CHORAL SONG (370-433): One of Euripides' most famous escape
    prayers; it responds to the preceding action by denouncing Pentheus' impi-
    ety and appealing to the spirit of Reverence. The song alternates by stanza
    between specific and general themes.
370: 'Holiness' (*Hosia*), apparently a cult word, is invoked as the opposite of Pen-
    theus' *hybris*. Although 'gods' of this kind were not formal objects of worship,
    the Greeks considered them real powers.

to put an end to anxieties
whenever the liquid joy of the clustered grapes
visits the feasts of the gods,
whenever the goblet casts sleep over men
during the ivy-wreathed festivities.   385

Antistrophe 1
Misfortune is the result
of unbridled mouths
and lawless folly.
The tranquil life and prudent thinking°   390
remain untossed by storms and hold the house together.°
For although the dwellers of heaven
inhabit the upper sky far away,
still they look down on human affairs.
So cleverness is not wisdom°   395
nor is it wise to think thoughts unfit for mortals.°
Life is short. Given such brevity
who would pursue ambitious ends
and lose what lies at hand?
These, in my opinion at least,   400
are the ways of madmen and evil counsellors.

Strophe 2
If only I could go to Cyprus
island of Aphrodite°
home of the Love gods
those erotic bewitchers of mortal minds   405
inhabitants of Paphos°
which the hundred mouths

390: **Tranquility and prudence:** The two key Dionysiac virtues for the chorus. These disaster-averting virtues contrast with Pentheus' rashness and frantic exertions. See Glossary, 'Dionysiac virtues.'

386-91: The chorus is alluding to the present quarrel between Pentheus and his grandfather Cadmus.

395: **The clever sophist's wisdom is folly:** 'Cleverness' translates *to sophon* ('the wise thing') which is 'a term of Dionysiac propaganda' (cp. 203) against the god's enemies (Oranje 164). From the chorus' point of view Pentheus' 'cleverness' is the opposite of their own Dionysiac 'wisdom' (*sophia*), which consists of reasoning well.

396: **Nothing in excess:** Violators of this adage inevitably suffer, e. g. Ajax, driven mad by Athena in Sophocles' play (761, 777) and Pentheus by Dionysus, in each case for thinking thoughts unfit for men.

403: Cyprus: birthplace of Aphrodite, goddess of sexuality, who was born from Cronus' severed penis.

406: Paphos: a town on the southwest coast of Cyprus, famous for its temple and altar to Aphrodite.

of a foreign river
fertilize without rain!°
If only I could go to exquisite Pieria°   410
home of the Muses°
sacred slope of Olympus!°
Take me there, Bromios, roaring spirit
who leads the Bacchic throng amid shouts of joy.
There the Graces live, and there Desire.°
And there it is lawful for the Bacchae to celebrate your mysteries.   415

Antistrophe 2
The god who is the son of Zeus
delights in festivities
and loves Peace, the goddess
who bestows bliss and nourishes youths.°
In equal measure he has given   420
to the rich and the humble°
so that mankind now possesses wine,
bringer of joy, banisher of care.
He hates the man whose concern is not this —
by day and by friendly night°   425
to live to the end a life of blessedness.
It is wise to keep one's heart and mind
at a distance from men of excess.
Whatever beliefs the common folk
have come to adopt and still practice,   430
these I would accept.

408-9: The 'foreign river' that fertilizes Paphos is the Nile. One theory about this
    passage is that Euripides believed that the Nile's strong currents deposited
    its rich silt on Cyprus' distant shores.
410: Pieria: The Muses' birthplace, a hilly area of Macedonia near Olympus. See
    Glossary, 'Mountains.'
411: Muses: The nine daughters of Zeus and Mnemosyne (Memory), goddesses of
    music and the arts. This connected them with Dionysus, god of music and
    theater. One tradition says they nursed baby Dionysus.
412: Olympus: a mountain range on the coast of Thessaly, separating Greece from
    Macedonia. The chorus wants to escape to Cyprus or Mt. Olympus because
    they represent the eastern and northern limits of the Greek world. And "since
    Dionysus is the god of the East and the North, it is natural that his worshippers
    should look eastward and northward for a place of refuge." (Dodds 123).
414: Graces (*Charites*): three daughters of Zeus who personified life's joys and all the
    pleasures of domain of Dionysus, with whom their cult was long associated.
419: Peace (*Eirene*, whence 'Irene') is associated with Dionysus because she, too,
    enriches human life. Her nurturing presence here makes the violence of the
    later songs all the more striking.
421: **Dionysus as the democratic god** *par excellence:* He gives wine to all.
425: Night is 'friendly' because Dionysus' mysteries are celebrated mostly in noctural
    darkness (485-86).

ACT II°

[Enter Soldier, stage left, with several guards leading the captured Stranger (Dionysus disguised); his hands are bound.]

Soldier°

Pentheus, we stand before you having captured this prey
after which you sent us; our mission has been accomplished.°   435
We found this wild beast tame. He didn't try to escape
but gave his hands to us willingly.
He didn't even turn pale or change his wine-flushed complexion.
Rather, laughing,° he bid us to bind and carry him off.
He even stood still so as to make my task easy.   440
Feeling ashamed I said to him: "Stranger, not willingly
do I arrest you but by the orders of Pentheus who sent me."
    Now as for the Theban Bacchae whom you shut up
and seized and bound in chains at the public jail,°
those women are gone, let loose and skipping off,   445
off to the mountain meadows, calling out to Bromios as their god.
The chains, of their own accord, came loose from the women's feet
and the keys unlocked the jailhouse doors without a human hand.
This man has come here to Thebes full of many miracles;°
but what happens next must be your concern, not mine.   450

Pentheus *[To his guards]*

Release this man's hands. Now that he's in my net
he won't be swift enough to escape me.
    [The guards remove the chains]
    Well, stranger, your body is indeed quite shapely, at least

---

ACT II (434-518) : **The apparent defeat of the Stranger** is presented in three phases (bound, un-bound, and re-bound): a] 434-450: he is brought on stage in chains b] 451-502: Pentheus temporarily releases his prisoner c] 503-518: Pentheus, in anger, chains the Stranger again, sending him off to prison.

434: In their last words (429-33) the chorus had voiced their acceptance of the beliefs of the 'common man.' With the soldier's entry at 434 we meet that 'common man' face to face.

435: Pentheus had sent these guards off at 352-57 in order to search the city and capture Dionysus.

439: **Dionysus wore a smiling mask;** so 380, 439, and 1020 suggest. See Glossary, 'Dionysus.'

444: The reference is to the Theban maenads whom Pentheus had jailed at 226-27.

449: *Bacchae* **as a miracle play:** Tiresias had attempted to prove Dionysus' existence by using rational arguments (272-318). Pentheus rejected them. Now he will be confronted with a series of miracles, first physical (449; cp. 667, 693, 716), then psychological, which present a different (i.e. non-rational) kind of proof of Dionysus' existence. The effect of the miracles on Pentheus is summarized by Dionysus at 787.

for enticing the women. And that's why you came to Thebes, isn't it?
Those long side-curls of yours show for sure you're no wrestler,° 455
rippling down your cheeks, infected with desire.
And you keep your skin white by deliberate contrivance,
not exposed to the sun's rays but protected by the shade,
hunting Aphrodite's pleasures with your beauty.°
First, then, tell me who you are and from what family. 460

The Stranger
I have no hesitation about this. It's easy to tell.
Surely you've heard of the flowering mountains of Tmolus.

Pentheus°
I have. They circle round the city of Sardis.°

The Stranger
I am from there and Lydia is my fatherland.

Pentheus
And from what source do you bring these rites to Greece? 465

The Stranger
Dionysus himself, the son of Zeus, sent me.

Pentheus
And does some local Zeus exist *there*, one who begets new gods?°

The Stranger
No, we have the same Zeus who yoked Semele *here* in Thebes.

Pentheus
And was it in a dream or face to face in daylight that he forced you
   into his service?

The Stranger
It was face to face. He looked at me, I at him.° And he gave me his
   sacred rites freely. 470

455: Because it gave the opponent a grip, long hair was considered a liability in
   wrestling.
455-59: This elaborate physical description suggests that Dionysus' *mask* reflected
   his effeminate beauty.
463-508: A two-part dialogue of alternating single lines [called *sticho-mythia*; see
   Glossary]. a) 463-491: Pentheus interrogates Dionysus, testing out what he
   has heard about the Stranger b) 492-508: Dionysus interrogates Pentheus,
   teasing out various punitive measures from him. Both parts of this dialogue
   (the play's longest) climax in frustration for Pentheus (cp. Oranje 55).
463: Sardis: Capital of Lydia (in Asia Minor) and a famous seat of Cybele's worship.
467: Pentheus' sarcastic implication is that the real Zeus is Greek, not some Asian
   imitation.
470: **The Stranger's initiation into Dionysus' rites:** In this face to face encounter
   the initiate becomes a virtual mirror of the god, an incarnate visual double,
   which indeed, as we know, the Stranger is.

Pentheus
And those rites—in your view, what form do they take?

The Stranger
That is forbidden knowledge for any mortals who are not Bacchae.

Pentheus
And what benefit does it hold for those who sacrifice?

The Stranger
It is unlawful for you to hear but the benefit is worth knowing.

Pentheus
You coined that answer cleverly so that I might wish to hear.°   475

The Stranger
On the contrary. For the rites of the god hate the man who practices impiety.°

Pentheus
Since you say that you saw the god clearly, what form did he take?

The Stranger
Whatever form he wanted. It wasn't for me to dictate that!°

Pentheus
Very clever, these empty-worded evasions of yours.

The Stranger
To the ignorant man, any speaker of wisdom will seem foolish.   480

Pentheus
Did you come here first to introduce your god?

The Stranger
No, every one of the foreigners dances these rites.°

Pentheus
That's because they're much more foolish than the Greeks.

The Stranger
In this case, at least, they're wise, though their customs are different.°

475: "The first admission of a reluctant curiosity that will grow into an obsession." (Kirk 63)
476: Impiety is a charge made three times (490, 502) by the Stranger against Pentheus. In 399 B.C. the same accusation was brought against Socrates and led to his death (Plato *Apology* 35d).
478: **Dionysus as the god of self-transformation:** cp. 4, 53-4, 920-22, 1017-19.
482: The vast extent of Dionysus' religious control in Asia was outlined at lines 13-19.
484: Multi-culturalism and the sophists: "The recognition that different cultures have different codes of behaviour and that the Greek code is not

Pentheus

Do you celebrate these sacred rites at night or in the day?   485

The Stranger

At night mostly, since darkness induces devotion.

Pentheus

No, darkness is devious and corrupts women.

The Stranger

Even in the day someone could devise shameful deeds.

Pentheus

You'll pay a penalty for your evil sophistries.

The Stranger

And you for your ignorance and impiety toward the god.   490

Pentheus

How bold this bacchus!° What a gymnast with words!

The Stranger

Tell me what I must suffer. What terrible deed you will inflict on me?

Pentheus

First I'll cut off those luxurious curls of yours.

The Stranger

My hair is sacred. I'm grooming it for the god.

Pentheus

And furthermore, hand over that thyrsus you're holding.   495

The Stranger

If you want it, you take it. This wand I carry belongs to Dionysus.°

---

necessarily...the best is one of the advances in thought due to the sophistic movement."(Dodds 138) See Glossary, 'Sophist.'

491: **'How bold this bacchus!'** A fine (unconscious) irony since 'this bacchus' before Pentheus is indeed Bacchus (cp. 622, 1020). But he has no clue. This passage (491-502) is full of irony as the god toys with his victim. (Seaford 1996, 189) See Glossary, 'Irony.'

493-96: Does Pentheus cut the Stranger's hair? Probably not: "...such a crudely blasphemous action would surely be given more explicit commentary in the words: rather, the impression is reinforced that the acceptance or rejection of the god can be made through [his] material symbols." (Taplin 98)

Pentheus [apparently backing off the challenge]
And we'll lock you up in prison.

The Stranger
The god himself will set me free whenever I wish.

Pentheus
Yes, when you call him, that is, from your jail cell beside the other
Bacchae!

The Stranger
Even now he is nearby and sees what I am suffering.   500

Pentheus
Well, where? To *my* eyes, at least, he's invisible.

The Stranger
Right where I am. But because you're so impious you can't see him.

Pentheus [to his soldiers]
Guards, seize this man. He insults me and Thebes.

The Stranger
From a wise man to fools, I order them not to bind me.

Pentheus
And I order them to bind you. I have more power than you!   505

The Stranger
You don't know what your life is — neither what you're doing nor
who you are.°

Pentheus
I am Pentheus, son of Agave and of my father Echion.°

The Stranger
Indeed you are and that name spells your misfortune.°

506: **Limits of knowledge:** Dionysus' riddle-like accusation recalls the all-too-ac-
curate jab of the seer Tiresias at another proud Theban king: "Though you
have eyes, you see neither where you are in evil nor where you live nor with
whom you share your house!" (*Oedipus the King* 412)
507: **Pentheus' blindness:** The literalness of his response (i.e. giving his own name
and his parents') underscores the king's striking ignorance of what he is doing (by binding the Stranger) and of who he is as a man (by thinking he has
power over the Stranger).
508: Dionysus puns on Pentheus' name as Tiresias had at 367; see Glossary,
'Pentheus' name.'

48

Pentheus [*To his soldiers*]

    Get out of here! Lock him up near the horse stables
    so that he sees only pitch darkness.   510

    [*To the Stranger*]
    Do your dancing there!

    [*The choristers start beating on their drums as the guards handcuff the Stranger*]
        And as for these women you've brought
    as collaborators in your evil deeds, either we'll sell them
    or I'll keep them as family possessions, slaves at my looms, after, that is,
    I've stopped their hands from banging out that rat-a-tat-tat on their
        drums.°

The Stranger

    I'm ready to go. For whatever is not fated, I'm not fated to suffer.   515
    But know well that as a punishment for these insults
    Dionysus will pursue you — the very god you claim doesn't exist.
    Since when you wrong us, it is him you throw into chains.

    [*The Stranger is lead off by the soldiers into the palace, followed by Pentheus.*]

Chorus of Asian Bacchae°
Strophe 1

    Hail, daughter of Achelous,°
    venerable Dirce,° happy maiden,   520
    since you once washed Zeus' infant son
    in your streams
    when Zeus, his sire, snatched him
    from the undying flame and hid the child
    in his own thigh, shouting out   525
        "Go, Dithyrambus,°

514: This is the first time that Pentheus takes notice of the chorus in the orchestra (cp. 55-61). That he actually threatens the chorus is quite extraordinary. Theatrical convention prevents him from executing his threat but the incident reveals again his *modus operandi*, namely force. He had already jailed the Theban maenads (226-27) but they escaped miraculously (443-48); the lesson did not register.

THIRD CHORAL SONG (519-75): Reacts to the preceding action and registers the growing wrath of the Bacchae at Pentheus and his threat to imprison them (which could not be carried out since stage conventions virtually dictated that the chorus remain in the orchestra). Dionysus' wilder aspects, which had been largely ignored in the first two odes, begin to emerge here.

519: Achelous: A river in west central Greece, the country's largest and so 'parent' to the others.

520: Dirce: The small river in the western quarter of Thebes.

526: '**Dithyrambus**': A sacred name for Dionysus. Euripides puns on the word's etymology, i. e. "he who came *twice* (*di*-) to the *doors* (*thyra*-) of birth." The dithyramb was Dionysus' special song, performed by choruses at revelries of wine, music, and wild abandonment. See Glossary, 'Dithyramb.'

enter this male womb of mine.
I hereby reveal you to Thebes, Bacchic child,
where you shall be called Dithyrambus from the manner of your birth."
But you, O blessed Dirce, reject me   530
though you have my ivy-crowned
bands of revellers on your banks.
Why do you spurn me? Why do you flee?
Yet one day soon — I swear by the grape-clustering
delights of Dionysus' vine —   535
one day soon you will take heed of Bromios.

Antistrophe 1
Pentheus reveals
his earth-born descent,
sprung from the serpent,
Pentheus whom earth-born Echion,   540
the Snake-Man, begot
as a fierce-faced monster
not a mortal man
but like a murderous Giant who wrestles the gods.°
Soon he will bind me,   545
Bromios' servant, in a noose.
Already he detains my fellow-reveller
inside the palace
hidden in a dark prison.
Son of Zeus, Dionysus,   550
do you see this, how your proclaimers
struggle against oppression?
Come down from Mt. Olympus, lord,
brandishing your golden thyrsus!
Restrain the hybris of this murderous man!   555

Epode°
Where, then, on beast-nourishing Mt. Nysa,°
are you, Dionysus, leading with your thyrsus
the revelling bands?

544: The chorus compare Pentheus' earth-born descent (cp. 264n.) to the chthonic
    descent of the giants who fought against the Olympian gods. Like the mon-
    strous Giants, Pentheus is a symbol of *hybris*.
Epode (556-75): Where is Dionysus to be found? The chorus' geographical inquiry
    seems to move north from Thebes to Thrace, i.e. from Mt. Nysa (probably in
    Boeotia, near Mt. Helicon) to Mt. Parnassus (in Phocis) to Mt. Olympus (in
    Thessaly) to Pieria (in southern Macedonia) to the rivers Axios and Lydias
    (in eastern Macedonia). [Leinieks 192]
556: Nysa: A mystical mountain that travelled wherever the god's cult did. See
    Glossary, 'Mountains.'

Or where on the Corcycian peaks of Mt. Parnassus?°
Or perhaps in the thickly-wooded lairs   560
of Mt. Olympus where once
Orpheus playing the lyre
gathered together the trees with his music
gathered together the wild animals?°
O blessed Pieria,   565
Euios° worships you and will come
to dance together with bacchic revelries.
He will lead his whirling maenads
after crossing the swift-flowing Axios   570
and the river Lydias, father of happiness
and bestower of prosperity to mortals.°
It is Lydias' sparkling waters,
so I've heard, which fertilize
that land and make it famed for horses.°   575

ACT III°

[The stage is completely empty and silent. Suddenly from offstage °]

THE VOICE (of Dionysus)°
Io!
Hear my voice, hear it!°
Io Bacchae, io Bacchae!

559: Parnassus: A mountain near the Gulf of Corinth, towering over Delphi. See
    Glossary, "Mountains."
561-64: Orpheus' magical music. This famous Thracian singer enchanted both the
    animate and inanimate worlds. Like Dionysus, he brought joy and unity.
566: Euios is a ritual name for Dionysus; see 67n.
572: Axios and Lydias: two Macedonian rivers running into the Thermaic Gulf in
    the northwest Aegean Sea.
575: Macedonia was famous for breeding fine horses; they appear on the coinage of
    her Hellenizing king, Archelaus, who invited Euripides to live at his court at
    Aegae around 408 B.C.
ACT III (576-861): Structural and thematic center of the *Bacchae*. Three main parts:
    a) 'palace miracles' (576-656); b) first messenger scene (657-786); c) tempting
    of Pentheus (787-861). The messenger scene is the center-piece, surrounded
    by two shorter episodes. The famous first episode (itself divided into three
    parts) contains a series of *supernatural* events which constitute the 'palace
    miracles'; a) the earthquake which shakes the palace (583-93, 623); b) Pentheus'
    hallucinations about the bull, the burning palace, and the light (615-31); c)
    the blazing of Zeus' lightning at Semele's tomb (594-99, 623-24); d) the (off-
    stage) collapse of the stable in which Dionysus had been jailed (633-34).
576: **Voice of god:** "Nowhere else in Greek tragedy is a god heard calling from off-
    stage, let alone accompanied by thunder and lightning." (Taplin 120)
576-603: **Lyric Dialogue #1:** The *Bacchae* features three *sung* dialogues (cp. 1024-42,
    1168-99). All three immediately follow a choral ode and are intensely emo-

Chorus-Leader [*in the orchestra*]
    Who is here, who is it?
    From where does the voice of Euios summon me?

THE VOICE
    Io! Again I speak,   580
    the son of Semele, the son of Zeus!

Chorus-Leader
    Io! Master, master!
    Come into our revelling band,
    O Bromios, Bromios!

THE VOICE
    Shake the very foundation of this world, august Goddess
       of Earthquakes!   585

Chorus-Leader
    Ah, ah!
    Look how quickly Pentheus' palace
    will be shaken to its fall!
    Dionysus is in the palace.
    Worship him!   590

Part of the Chorus [*in response*]
    We worship him.
    Didn't you see the stone lintels reeling, breaking apart
    there on the columns?° Bromios, the roaring lord of thunder, is here,
    raising his ritual shout of triumph in the palace.

THE VOICE [*calling on the Earthquake goddess*]
    Fire up the blazing torch of lightning!
    Burn it, burn the palace of Pentheus!   595

Another Part of the Chorus
    Ah, ah! Don't you see the fire, don't you see it
    around Semele's sacred tomb,
    the thunder-hurled flame
    that long ago Zeus' bolt left behind?°
    Throw your trembling bodies to the ground!   600

---

    tional sequences which alternate between an actor *singing* from the stage and
    the chorus (or chorus-leader) *singing* from the orchestra. Here the theme is
    Dionysus' liberation of his band of maenadic worshippers from Pentheus.
576: In the last stanza of the preceding song (556-75) the chorus had invoked
    Dionysus. His off-stage cry to the Bacchae here seems designed to be under-
    stood as the god's reply to that petition of his worshippers.
592-93: **Was the earthquake represented on stage?** Given the simplicity of fifth
    century stage mechanisms, this scene was probably meant to be conjured in
    the mind's eye. See Glossary, 'Earthquake.'
596-99: At this point flames probably shot forth from Semele's smouldering tomb
    (cp. 8; 623).

Maenads, throw your bodies down!°
For the king, Zeus' son, will come rushing
upon this house, turning it upside down.
*[The terrified chorus throw themselves onto the orchestra floor; perhaps a
crash is heard. Enter the Stranger from the palace]* °

The Stranger
Women of Asia, are you so paralyzed with fear
that you've fallen to the ground? It seems you felt   605
the Bacchic god shaking apart Pentheus' house.
Come on, lift up your bodies! Take courage! Cast off your trembling!

Chorus-Leader
O greatest light of our bacchic revelry! Euoi!
How delighted I am to see you! Before I felt such a deep loneliness.°

The Stranger
Had you reached despair when I was summoned,   610
thinking I would fall in Pentheus' dark dungeons?

Chorus-Leader
Indeed we had. Who would have protected us if you had met misfortune?
Tell me, how were you freed after meeting that impious man?

The Stranger
I saved myself easily and without any toil.

Chorus-Leader
But didn't he bind your hands in tight nooses?   615

601: **Uniqueness of *chorus* being called 'maenads':** The *Theban* women are called
'maenads' 13 times but "this is the only place in which a word beginning
main- ('mad') describes the chorus." (Seaford 1996, 199) This is because they
are so agitated during the earthquake: "It is their intense experience of fear
which makes them *mainades* (madwomen) here."(Leinieks 78, 108) See Glossary, 'Maenads.'

604 ff: **Arresting stagecraft:** "The music stops, the devotees lie prostrate: this is the
moment for an epiphany above the palace. Instead, 'the stranger', the holy
man, walks calmly out of the door. Something of the agitation lingers on in
the trochaic scene which follows (604-41); but by the time Pentheus re-enters
(642), Dionysus wears the same amused impassivity as before. The tableau
moment at 603 is, in a way, an anti-climax; but it conveys most impressively
Dionysus' blend of brute power and gentle humour. Pentheus has no eye for
it, and the humour will have to become brutal." (Taplin 120).

604-41: **Change of meter:** The tempo changes dramatically here to a fast 'running'
meter (trochaic tetrameter) to convey the excitement of what happens in the
immediate aftermath of the 'earthquake.'

609: **Choral reaction to the liberation of the Stranger.** The Bacchae move from fear
(604), trembling (607), loneliness (609) and despair (610) — all the result of
the earthquake and fire at Semele's tomb — to joy (609) at seeing the great
light (608) which they identify with the god. Their experience of the initiation-
like ritual into the Dionysiac mysteries stands in stark contrast to Pentheus'
experience at 616ff.

The Stranger
    In just this I mocked him. He thought he had bound me
when in fact he never even laid a hand on us but fed on his hopes.
Finding a bull° in the stables where he had led me as a prisoner
he threw nooses around its knees and hooves,
breathing out fury, sweating profusely from his body,   620
gnashing his teeth into his lips. But I, sitting calmly nearby,
just watched. In the meantime Bacchus came
and shook the palace, kindling a flame on his mother's tomb.
When Pentheus saw this, thinking the palace was burning,
he rushed to and fro, ordering his servants to bring water.   625
Every slave helped in the task but they all labored in vain.°
Imagining that I had escaped, he gave up this toil
and darted into the dark house with his dagger drawn. Then Bromios,
as it seems to me at least, since I speak only my opinion, made a light in
the courtyard.° Chasing eagerly after it, Pentheus rushed forward 630
and tried to stab the shining [image], thinking he was slaying me.
Besides these humiliations, Bacchus outraged him in other ways too.
He smashed the building to the ground. Everything lies shattered
so that now he sees the most bitter consequences of trying to chain me.°
From weariness he has dropped his sword and lies exhausted.   635
Though only a man, he dared to fight a god. Calmly leaving the palace,
I have come to you, giving no thought to Pentheus.°

618: **Bull imagery** recurs at 100, 920, 1017, 1159; Dionysus is god of the bull. Compare
    the frightening apparition of the bull (symbol of male sexuality) that destroys
    the protagonist in *Hippolytus* (1214).
626: They labored in vain; the house was *not* on fire; Pentheus only *thought* so (616,
    624, 631).
630: **Why does Pentheus mistake 'a light' for his prisoner?** Because in ancient ini-
    tiation ritual the mystic light appearing in the (Hades-like) darkness seems to
    have been identified with the god himself. So here Pentheus rushes from the
    dark house (628; cp. the *dark* stables at 510, 611) to the courtyard where he sees
    the *light* (630; cp. 608 and 1083) created by the god, which light he mistakes
    for a man— just as he mistook the bull for a man at 619-22. This young king
    "embodies not only the ordeals of the initiand, but also, as the god's enemy,
    the negation of the desired ritual process. He rejects and attacks even the
    light in the darkness, and persists in his hostile and confused ignorance."
    (Seaford 1981, 256-57) [Most editors prefer the emendation *phasma*, which
    means 'phantom'; I follow the manuscript's *phôs*, 'light;' so also Seaford (1996)
    202 and Leinieks 366.]
634: Dionysus is here scorning Pentheus' earlier boast (357) that the Stranger would
    have a 'bitter' bacchic revelry in Thebes.
616-37: **Pentheus' failed initiation into the Dionysiac mysteries:** The king's ordeals
    as he tries to tie up the bull resemble those of the initiand in the mysteries.
    See Glossary, 'Pentheus' failed initiation.'

Hush! I hear a trampling of boots in the palace. Soon, I think,
he'll be at the door. What in the world will he say after all this?
No matter. I'll remain calm even if he comes out breathing fury.°   640
For it is the part of a wise man to employ a controlled and gentle
temper.

[Enter Pentheus from the palace, panting heavily]°

Pentheus
I have suffered terribly! The stranger has escaped me
even though I had just forced him into chains.
Hey! Hey!
He is right here. What is this?   645

[Turning to the Stranger]
What are you doing in front of my house? How did you get outside?

The Stranger
Slow down. Calm your anger.

Pentheus
How did you escape those chains? How did you get out here?

The Stranger
Didn't I say, or didn't you hear — that someone will set me free?°

Pentheus
Who? The answers you give are always strange.   650

The Stranger
He who grows the rich-clustering vine for mortals.

Pentheus
............*[one or several lines missing]°*

640: For the third time in this speech Dionysus' calmness is contrasted with Pentheus'
    tempestuousness.
642-56: **Pentheus' second meeting with the Stranger.** "This short passage of dia-
    logue makes the transition from the Palace Scene to the Messenger Scene,
    being linked to the former by its subject, to the latter by its metre. It does not
    directly advance the action: its function (as 639 suggests) is to show the dawn-
    ing of a new relationship between the antagonists, brought about by the
    strange happenings behind the scenes. Pentheus' bluster cannot wholly con-
    ceal his bewilderment and inner dread: in the face of the uncanny he is be-
    ginning to lose his nerve. And the Stranger for his part speaks now for the
    first time with a hint of supernatural authority (647)." (Dodds 156-57)
649: The Stranger had said at line 498 that 'the god himself' would free him.
651a: Textual uncertainty: After 651 there seems to be a gap in which Pentheus said
    something sarcastic (cp. 499) such as *"And the god released you in order that you
    would destroy the women in their drunkenness?"* (supplement by Oranje 71).
    Some scholars, less convincingly, place the lacuna after 652 and attribute the
    lost line(s) to Dionysus. Seaford (1996) argues that there is no lacuna and
    gives 652-53 to Pentheus: "This (supposed) good is in fact a reproach to
    Dionysus. I order every tower to be locked in a circle."

The Stranger

Look, now you've insulted Dionysus for what he's right to be proud of.

[Exit two guards, one down each side-ramp.]

Pentheus *[turning to his guards]*

I command you to lock every gate in the encircling rampart.°

The Stranger

But why? Don't gods scale even walls?

Pentheus

Clever, very clever indeed, except in what you should be clever!   655

The Stranger

In whatever I must be especially clever, in that I am indeed naturally so.°
First, however, listen to this messenger here and learn from him.°
He has come from the mountains to bring you news.°
Don't worry. We will stay right here; we won't try to escape.

[Enter the first messenger, a herdsman from Mt. Cithaeron, hastily from stage left.]

Messenger #1

Pentheus, ruler of this Theban land,   660
I have come from Mt. Cithaeron
where the bright shafts of white snow fell incessantly.

Pentheus

What message have you come to deliver with such urgency?

Messenger #1

I have just seen the august Bacchae.° Stung with frenzy
they shot forth from this land bare-footed.   665
I have come desiring to tell you and the city, my lord,
what strange feats they do, greater than miracles.
But I want to know whether I can speak freely to you
about what happened there or whether I must reef in my report.
For I fear the swiftness of your mind, my lord;   670
it is quick to anger and too much that of a king.

653: Pentheus' purpose is to prevent the Stranger from joining the Theban maenads on Mt. Cithaeron.

655-56: The fourfold repetition of 'clever' (*sophos*) highlights the opposing opinions about 'wisdom.'

657: **Plot changes direction:** At this point the first main action, Dionysus' escape and liberation, has come to an end and the second action, Dionysus' vengeance on Pentheus, begins.

658: **Dionysus as director within the play:** "How does Dionysus *know* that this is a messenger from the mountains? The hint is sown that Dionysus himself has 'arranged' this messenger-speech as an opportunity for Pentheus to see the truth, in fact one of a series of opportunities." (Taplin 57)

664: The messenger emphasizes (664, 680, 693, 760) that he was an eye-witness of the reported events.

Pentheus

Speak openly since you won't be punished by me
no matter what your story. [It isn't fitting to be angry with just men.]
The more frightening your account of the Bacchae
the more severe will be the punishment   675
of the man who taught his wiles to those women.

Messenger #1°

Our herds of young cattle were just climbing
towards the upland pastures.
As the sun let loose its rays to warm the earth
I see three bands of female choruses.°   680
Autonoe was the leader of one group,
your mother Agave of another, and Ino of a third.
They were all sound asleep, relaxed in their bodies,
some leaning their backs on fir-tree foliage,
others resting their heads on oak leaves,   685
they were scattered on the ground haphazardly but modestly
and not, as you claim, drunk with wine and flute music°
and hunting down Aphrodite's delights on solo missions in the forest.
    Then your mother, standing up amidst the Bacchae,
shouted a ritual cry and roused their bodies from sleep   690
after she had heard the bellowing of my horned oxen.
Throwing off the fresh sleep from their eyes
they sprang to their feet, a miracle of discipline to behold,
women young and old, and girls still unmarried.°
First they let their hair flow loose onto their shoulders   695
and tied up their fawnskins — those whose knot fastenings
had come undone — and bound tight the dappled hides
with snakes that licked their cheeks.°
Some, holding in their arms a fawn or wild wolf cubs,
offered them white milk — those who had just given birth   700

677-774: **First Messenger speech:** Laden with an air of mystery, it describes the
    magical powers of the Theban Bacchae on the mountain. Its main purpose is
    to persuade Pentheus to accept Dionysus and his female devotees (769-74).
680: Triads of maenads: Females associated with Dionysus in myth often appear
    in triplets: Cadmus' daughters are the most famous triad, each being leader
    of a *thiasos* (cult group).
687: Pentheus had made his claims about the drunkenness and lechery of the Bacchae
    at 221-25 (cp. 236-38); the messenger will correct Pentheus again at 712-13.
694: These are the women whom Dionysus had earlier (35-38) driven mad and
    onto Mt. Cithaeron.
698: The maenads' snakes (cp. 104, 767-8) are from the world of myth, not reality.
    No surviving literary source (except *Bacchae*) mentions snake handling as
    part of maenadic ritual. (Carpenter 111)

and whose breasts were still swollen,
having left their new-born at home.
They crowned themselves with wreaths of ivy
and oak and flowering evergreen creepers.
One woman, taking her thyrsus, struck it against a rock°
and from it a spring of fresh water leaps out.   705
Another struck her fennel wand against the ground
and for this woman the god sent forth a stream of wine.
As many as had a desire for white drink,
scraping through the earth with their sharp fingers
they got springing jets of milk. And from the ivy thyrsi   710
sweet streams of honey dripped.
So that if you had been present to see these things,°
the very god you now censure you would have pursued with prayers.

    We came together, cowherds and shepherds,
to wrangle with one another in our accounts   715
[debating their uncanny and miraculous deeds.]
Then some wanderer from the city with a knack for words
spoke to us all:

    "O you who dwell in the holy uplands
of the mountains, do you wish to hunt Agave,
Pentheus' mother, out from her bacchic revelry   720
and gain the king's favor?"

    His suggestion seemed reasonable
so we lay in ambush in the thickets, concealing ourselves
in the foliage. At the appointed hour each woman
began to wave her thyrsus in the bacchic dancing,
calling out with multitudinous voice on Bromios as 'Iacchus,'°   725
Lord of Cries, the son of Zeus. The whole mountain and all its wild
   creatures
joined the Bacchic revelry and everything was roused to running.°

704-11: **Dionysus as god of liquid nature:** "Dionysus is a miraculous wine-maker
    (*Homeric Hymn* 7.35), and his power is transmitted to those possessed by him
    when they wield his magic rod. Since he is 'lord of all liquid nature' (Plutarch
    Isis and Osiris 35), his rod can also, like Moses', draw water from the rock,
    and its power extends likewise to the two other liquids which Nature gives
    to man—milk and honey." (Dodds 163). The miracle of water, wine, milk,
    and honey was foreshadowed at 141-43.

712: The messenger's personal appeal actively draws Pentheus into his account
    (cp. 737, 740, 748), thus making the king more curious and eager to see the
    reported miracles for himself.

725: Iacchus: A mystic name of Dionysus at Athens and Eleusis; see Glossary,
    'Iacchus.'

726-27: A mystical union of god, woman, and nature: "These strange and beautiful
    words startled ancient critics as an example of imaginative boldness verging
    on extravagance." (Dodds 166)

Agave happens to jump close by me
and I leapt out hoping to seize her,
deserting the thicket where I was hiding myself.   730
But she shrieked:
    "O my running hounds,
    we are being hunted by these men here. Follow me!
    Follow me, armed like soldiers with your thyrsi at hand!"°
Only by fleeing did we avoid
being torn to pieces by the Bacchae;°   735
but they attacked our grazing calves and not with swords in their
    hands.
You could have seen one of them, apart from the others, mauling with
    both hands
a young heifer with swelling udders, bellowing all the while;
and other women were ripping apart mature cows, shredding them up.
You could have seen ribs or a cleft hoof   740
being tossed up and down. Hanging from the fir trees
the ribs and hooves dripped bloody gore.
Bulls previously aggressive and tossing their horns in rage
now tumbled to the ground, their bodies dragged down
by the myriad hands of young women.   745
Their garments of flesh were ripped off
faster than you could have winked your royal eyes.
Like birds the women rose, racing in rapid flight
over the outstretched plains where Thebes' fruitful crop grows
along the streams of the Asopus river.°   750
Attacking Hysiae and Erythrae,°
nestled in the low hill country of Cithaeron,
like enemy soldiers they scattered things in every direction,
turning it all upside down. They snatched children from their homes.
And whatever they carried on their shoulders   755
was held fast without being fastened and didn't fall [to the black earth,
not bronze, not iron.] On their locks of hair

733: **Thyrsus as defensive weapon:** This line "recalls many early fifth-century de-
    pictions [on vases] of maenads using their thyrsoi to defend themselves
    against satyrs." (Carpenter 117)
735: **'Being torn to pieces'** (*sparagmos*): The appearance of this important noun here
    (735, 739) foreshadows a much more gruesome *sparagmos* (cp. 1127, 1135, 1220).
    See Glossary, 'Tearing-to-pieces.'
750: Asopus: A small river in Boeotia originating on Cithaeron near Plataea and
    flowing into the Gulf of Euboea. Running between Thebes (north) and
    Cithaeron (south), it separated Thebes and Plataea.
751: Hysiae and Erythrae: Boeotian villages in the Asopus river valley, eight miles
    south of Thebes. Hysiae was near Plataea, on the road to Athens; Erythrae
    was a little further east.

they carried fire and it did not burn them. And the villagers,
enraged at being plundered by the Bacchae, took to arms.
That was indeed a dreadful spectacle to behold, my lord.   760
For the men's sharp-pointed spears drew no blood from the maenads,
neither bronze nor iron [...], but the women, hurling thyrsi from their
   hands,
were wounding the villagers and turning them to flight.°
Women routed men, though not without some god's help.°
Back to that spot whence they had set out the Bacchae returned,   765
I mean to the very streams that the god had made spring up for them.
They washed off the blood while the snakes with their tongues
were licking from their skin the drops on their cheeks.°
   So this god — whoever he is — receive him, master,°
into our city since in other matters, too, they say   770
he is great but especially in this, so I hear,
because he gave to mortals the vine that stops pain.
If there were no more wine, then there is no more Aphrodite
nor any other pleasure for mankind.°

[Exit messenger, stage left]

Chorus-leader
   I am afraid to speak freely to the tyrant   775
but still it shall be said once and for all.°
Dionysus is inferior to none of the gods!

Pentheus
   Already it blazes up nearby like fire,
this insolent hybris of the Bacchae, a huge humiliation to Greeks.
But I must not hesitate.°   780

[turning to an attendant]

763: **Thyrsus as offensive weapon:** Once an instrument of worship, it here becomes
   an instrument of war. This duality expresses well the ambiguity of Dionysus'
   cult as practiced by the maenads.
764: **Sex role reversals** are important in the *Bacchae*; for maenads as *soldiers* cp. 733,
   753, 785-86.
767-68: Whose blood are the maenads washing off? Apparently it belongs to the
   cattle torn apart at 736-42 (Dodds 171).
769: The messenger's third and final warning to Pentheus to accept the god (cp.
   666-67, 712-13).
769-74: Messengers customarily end their speeches with gnomic statements (cp.
   1150-52).
776: The Chorus is not the only one afraid of Pentheus; the Messenger at 670 ex-
   pressed a similar fear.
780: **Effect of messenger speech on Pentheus:** It shifts his wrath to the Theban
   maenads whereas before it was focussed on the Stranger (674-76).

You there, go to the Electran gates.°
Order all the shield-bearing foot-soldiers
and riders of swift-footed horses to meet me there.
Call up my light infantry, too, and the archers.
We're going to march against the Bacchae
since this is too much to bear, that we suffer   785
what we suffer at the hands of women.°

[Exit attendant, stage right]

The Stranger

You do not obey me at all, Pentheus, even though you have heard my
   words.°
I have suffered badly at your hands
but still I say you ought not take up arms against a god.
Keep calm. Bromios will not endure any attempts to drive
   his Bacchae   790
from the mountains that ring out with cries of joy for him.

Pentheus

Don't lecture me! Since you've escaped despite being bound
won't you guard your freedom? Or shall I punish you again?

The Stranger

I would sacrifice to him rather than rage on,°

781: Pentheus intends to rally his troops at the gate of Electra. From that southern
   exit the army could march to Cithaeron. But the king's order is soon forgotten
   as a result of the plot taking a new direction.

786: **Humiliation by women**: A common fear of males in tragedy (*Antigone* 484-85).
   It is Pentheus' masculine pride that provokes his call to arms. See Glossary,
   'Shame Culture.'

787: **The Stranger's various 'proofs' of Dionysus' divinity:** Thus far Pentheus
   remains unpersuaded. At 789-809 the Stranger presents one last chance by
   offering to bring the maenads peacefully from Cithaeron to Thebes.

787-809: A two-part dialogue (first half = alternating *double* lines, second half =
   alternating *single* lines) in which the Stranger tries to dissuade Pentheus from
   hunting down the Bacchae: a) 787-801: you are fighting against *a god*. b) 802-
   809: I myself will bring the maenads here from the mountain without force.
   Both the Stranger's arguments fail to convince Pentheus (similarly 460-508);
   this failure will force Dionysus, at 810 ff., to devise a more drastic strategy
   for capturing his prey (cp. Oranje 77-80).

794: **Perils of anger:** The Stranger's counsel takes the form of a clever pun on the
   similar sounds of *thuô* (sacrifice) and *thumos* (anger, passion), a similarity
   that highlights the antithesis between the two notions. [Seaford 1996, 212].
   Pentheus is being warned about the dangers of his anger (*thumos*). Earlier
   the messenger had feared the suddenness of Pentheus' *thumos* (671). This
   problem of reason being blinded by emotion occurs elsewhere in Euripides. It is because of her *thumos* that Medea (431 B.C.) murders her children
   (1078-80): "I understand what pain I shall endure, but my anger (*thumos*) is
   stronger than my rational deliberations, anger which is indeed the cause of
   men's greatest pain."

kicking against the pricks, a man at war with god.°   795

Pentheus
Yes, I'll sacrifice but it will be the women's slaughter.° That's what
they deserve.
I'll stir up plenty of it in the valleys of Cithaeron.

The Stranger
You will be the ones fleeing, each and every one of you. And what a
disgrace,
to turn your bronze-forged shields before the wands of women.

Pentheus
Troublesome indeed is this stranger with whom we're entangled.   800
Whether tied up or not, he just won't keep quiet.

The Stranger
Sir, it is still possible to arrange these things well.°

Pentheus
By doing what? Being a slave to my slaves?

The Stranger
I'll bring the women here without using the force of weapons.

Pentheus
Alas! Now you're devising some trick against me!   805

The Stranger
What sort of trick, if I want to save you by my wiles?

Pentheus
You've made this compact with the Bacchae so you can revel with
them forever.

The Stranger
I have indeed made a compact — you can be sure of that — but it is
with the god.

Pentheus [*turning to one of his guards*]
You there, bring my weapons out here.°

[*Exit guard into palace; Pentheus turns to the Stranger*]
And you, stop talking!

795: **'Don't kick against the pricks'**: A warning: don't resist those more powerful
because your resistance will prove self-destructive.
796: Perverted sacrifice: It will indeed be 'the women's slaughter,' but *by* them, not
of them (see 1114). "As sacrifice is the ordered killing of animals, what Pentheus threatens is a perverted sacrifice, the disordered slaughter of human
victims... But Pentheus himself will be the victim of just such a perverted
sacrifice." [Seaford 1996, 212]
802: Is Dionysus' offer to resolve the conflict genuine (Seaford 1996, 212) or a sinister
mockery (Oranje 78)? If genuine, it emphasizes Pentheus' stubbornness.
809: Pentheus, frustrated, breaks off negotiations and again turns to force as a solu-
tion (similarly 503, 653).

The Stranger

Ah! °   810

Do you want to see those women sitting together in the mountains?°

Pentheus

Indeed I would. I'd give a vast weight of gold for that.

The Stranger

But why have you fallen into so great a passion for seeing them?°

Pentheus

I would be pained to see them drunk with wine.

The Stranger

But still you would see with pleasure things that are bitter to you? 815

Pentheus

Certainly I would — but in silence and sitting under the fir trees.

The Stranger

But they will track you down even if you go secretly.

Pentheus

Good point. I'd better go openly.

The Stranger

Shall we lead you then? Will you really venture on the journey?

Pentheus

Lead me as quickly as possible. I begrudge the time you're wasting. 820

The Stranger

Then put on this long dress of fine oriental linen.

Pentheus

What are you saying? Instead of being a man shall I join the ranks of
women?

810: **'Ah': The play's 'monosyllabic turning point'** (Taplin 158). This uncanny moment marks the beginning of the end for Pentheus who now comes under the
god's power and loses much of his ability to reason. The Greek word here is
'a', a strong but hard-to-define interjection. Formally it occupies its own line
and thus interrupts the swift single-line repartee. Though only momentary, the
break signals a portentous change in the plot's direction. Pentheus' obstinacy
has forced Dionysus to shift gears and, as line 811 indicates, to initiate a new
strategy, outlined more fully at 847-61.

811-48: **Dionysus' new plan:** He initiates now a second 'device' to prove his divinity; the first (driving the Theban women into a frenzy) has failed to convince
Pentheus. The second will be to punish Pentheus by driving him into a frenzy.
The scheme has two parts (cp. Oranje 82-85): a) getting Pentheus to go to the
mountain and *look at* the maenads (811, 819); b) agreeing to lead Pentheus to
the mountain, if he will *dress up* as a maenad (821 ff).

813: **Pentheus'** *passion* **to see the maenads:** The word for 'passion' here is *erôs*,
the strongest Greek noun for sexual desire. On its significance see Glossary,
'Pentheus' passion.'

822: Alternately: "Am I then to be *ritualized* from man to woman?" (Leinieks 51)

The Stranger
Yes. I fear they would kill you if you were seen as a man there.°

Pentheus
Another good point. You're a pretty clever fellow and have been right along.°

The Stranger
Dionysus instructed us fully in these matters.   825

Pentheus
How could your advice be successfully carried out?

The Stranger
I myself will dress you up once we've gone into the house.

Pentheus
In what kind of costume? A woman's? But I would be ashamed.°

The Stranger
Are you no longer so eager to be a spectator of the maenads?

Pentheus
This costume — what exactly do you propose to dress me in?   830

The Stranger
First I'll stretch out long the hair on your head.°

Pentheus
And the second feature of my adornment, what is that?

The Stranger
A dress down to your feet. And for your hair we have a headband.°

Pentheus
Will you add anything else to my outfit?

The Stranger
Yes, a thyrsus for your hand and a spotted fawnskin.   835

Pentheus
I couldn't bear to put on a female costume.

823-24: **Why does Pentheus disguise himself as a woman?** Here the primary reason is physical safety; he must look like a maenad lest he be killed. See Glossary, 'Pentheus as transvestite.'

811-24: **Pentheus' sudden change of mind:** In the space of just fourteen verses the Stranger virtually transforms Pentheus from a man into a woman.

828: Pentheus' shame reveals the conflict between his manly pride and his passion to see the maenads.

831: Pentheus' long hair: The reference seems to be either to a wig (such as the male actors of the maenad chorus wore) or to the releasing of long hair held fast by a headband.

833: Pentheus' headband and its ritual significance: The headband, associated with Lydia and usually worn by women to bind their hair, consisted of a piece of cloth wrapped around the head. It seems to have been part of Dionysiac ritual dress, possibly a sign of dedication to the god's service. (Dodds 177)

The Stranger

But you will spill blood if you engage the Bacchae in battle.°

Pentheus

Good point. I must first go and spy them out.°

The Stranger

That is certainly wiser than to hunt down evil by means of evil.°

Pentheus

But how will I avoid the notice of the Cadmeans as I pass through the
  city?   840

The Stranger

We will take the deserted streets. I'll lead you.

Pentheus

Anything is better than being laughed at by the Bacchae.°

The Stranger

Once we've gone into the house, [we'll make the necessary arrangements.]°

Pentheus

[Hold on!] I'll do the deciding about what seems best.

The Stranger

Very well. Whatever you decide, my course of action is prepared.

Pentheus

I think I'll go in. For either I will march with weapons°   845

837: Textual ambiguity: Does Pentheus understand the spilt blood to be his own or
  that of the Bacchae (cp. 796)? If it is the former, that would help explain his
  decision in the next line to desist from battle.

838: **Pentheus' change of mind:** Pentheus had intended to spill the blood of the
  Bacchae (796, 809) but now he will *spy* on them instead. As Seaford (1996, 215)
  notes, "it is psychologically apt that it is by a military intention that Pentheus
  overcomes his reluctance to wear female dress."

839: What does the Stranger mean? Two possibilities: a) "Don't ask for trouble by
  inflicting it," i.e. beware lest you become the hunted rather than the hunter (cp.
  228, 796). In this case, the first evil refers to the violence inflicted on Pentheus
  as a result of the second evil, his inflicting of violence on the maenads. b)
  "Don't hunt down one social evil at the cost of another." In this case, the first
  evil is the activity of the maenads on Cithaeron, the second evil is Pentheus'
  shedding of their blood. (Dodds 179)

842: The point here is not that Pentheus is afraid of being laughed at by the Bacchae
  in the streets of Thebes when he is disguised in a woman's costume; they
  are, after all, on the mountain and at this point he is still in the city. What he
  fears is allowing the Bacchae to triumph over him; that would be the ultimate
  mockery. Hence his decision to spy on them.

843-44: Text and attribution of lines are uncertain; the brackets enclose the most
  accepted supplements.

845: Pentheus' third and final threat to take by force the maenads on Mt. Cithaeron
  (cp. 784, 809).

or I'll obey your advice.

[Exit Pentheus into palace]

The Stranger°
Women, the man stands within the cast of our net.
He will come to the Bacchae and pay the penalty of death!
Dionysus, now the deed is yours — for you are not far off.
Let us punish him! First put him outside his mind.   850
Instill a light-headed frenzy.° Since, if he reasons well,
he definitely won't be willing to dress in a woman's costume.
But if he drives off the road of reason, he will dress up.
I want the Thebans to mock him°
as we parade him through the city in his dainty disguise,°   855
after those terrifying threats of his.°
I'll go and dress Pentheus up in the very adornments
he'll wear to Hades after being slain by his mother's hands.
He will come to know Dionysus, the son of Zeus,
that he is, in the ritual of initation,° a god most terrifying,   860
but for mankind a god most gentle.°

[Exit the Stranger into the palace]

846: "I'll *obey*" could also, because of its ambiguous verbal form in Greek, carry a very
    different (and more ironic) meaning, namely "I'll *suffer* (by your advice)."
847-61: **Thematic prologue to second half of play.** This fifteen line speech summa-
    rizes the god's plan of revenge - a plan that will drive the rest of the action.
851: **'Light-headed frenzy':** It is this dizzying mental delusion (*lyssa*; cp. 977, 981)
    as well as his new role as a Dionysiac initiand that will bring about Pentheus'
    change of personality.
854: **Laughter as a weapon:** Greek 'shame culture' dictated that one man's victory
    came at another's expense. Being mocked meant 'losing face' and was to be
    avoided at all costs. See Glossary, 'Laughter.'
855: **Pentheus' female disguise:** Why does he cross-dress? For reasons of safety
    (821-23) and because transvestism is a well-known feature of initiation rites,
    depriving the initiand of his previous identity so he can assume a new one.
    See Glossary, 'Pentheus as transvestite.'
856: Earlier Pentheus had mocked Dionysus' 'girlish shape' (353); now Dionysus
    returns the favor, mocking Pentheus' 'womanly shape.'
860: **The terror of Dionysus in ritual initiation.** Dionysus is for mankind "most
    gentle" but for his initiands "most terrifying" because they must undergo
    the terrors of ritual death that preceded the spiritual rebirth of the Dionysiac
    mysteries. [I have translated the important and controversial phrase *en telei*
    in 860 as "in the initiation of ritual." (Seaford 1996, 217)]. Other possible in-
    terpretations: "that Dionysus was born a god *with a god's authority*" or "that
    Dionysus is *by turns* a most awesome and a most gentle god to mortals."
860-61: **The god's elusive doubleness:** This powerful conclusion to Act III un-
    derscores the god's frightening ambiguity (i.e., gentility and terror). It also
    foreshadows the theme of the following ode whose *strophe* stresses the lib-
    erating quality of Dionysus and whose *antistrophe* foregrounds his potential
    vengefulness.

Chorus of Asian Bacchae°
Strophe 1

Shall I ever move
my white feet in the all-night dances
breaking forth into Bacchic frenzy
tossing my neck back   865
into the night's dewy air
like a fawn° sporting amid the green delights of the meadow
when it has escaped the fearful hunt
eluding the ring of watchmen
beyond their well-woven nets   870
as the shouting hunter
incites his speedy hounds?
Swift as a storm-wind the fawn toils, races,
bounds toward the plain alongside the river
delighting in the wilderness devoid of men   875
delighting in the young shoots of the leaf-shaded forest.°

Refrain

What good is mere cleverness? Or rather, what god-given gifts
bring more honor to mortals
than to hold the hand of mastery
over the head of the enemy?°   880
Whatever is honorable is dear always.°

FOURTH CHORAL SONG (862-911): This passionate ode, sung to the rhythms of
traditional cult hymns, expresses the chorus' restored hope that, as a result
of the palace miracles, they will be free to honor Dionysus without fear of
Pentheus, who must be punished. The hymn separates the Stranger's preceding prediction of victory from the victory itself.

867: Maenads as fawns: a natural image since they are wearing fawnskin costumes;
cp. 111n.

876: The fawn's non-stop flight has purposive motion: escaping from the meadow
toward water of the river (where the dogs would lose the scent) and finally
to the safety of the deep forest.

877-81: **A controversial refrain:** Textual uncertainty has resulted in two different
interpretations of the chorus' attitude toward their enemies. I have followed
Seaford (1994, 402-5) and Leinieks (1996, 371). The other (opposite) interpretation: "What is cleverness? Or rather, what better gift of the gods to mortals
exists than to hold a stronger hand over the head of enemies? What is good is
dear always." (Dodds 186) This latter interpretation seems somewhat at odds
with the following stanza where the emphasis is on the gods, not mortals,
punishing the enemy.

879-80: **The head of enemies:** Foreshadows Pentheus' fate and also alludes to the
main tenet of Greek moral thought from Homer to Plato, namely 'to help one's
friends and harm one's enemies.' See Glossary, 'Helping friends.'

881: "What is fine is dear always." An old proverb; here it means that what is good
is the wisdom of the Dionysiac worshipper. Such wisdom (cp. 1150) leaves
revenge on one's enemies to the god. (Leinieks 372)

Antistrophe 1

It starts out slowly
but still the strength of the gods
is trustworthy. And it punishes
those mortals who honor foolish arrogance   885
and those who, in the madness
of their opinions, do not extol things divine.
The gods cunningly conceal
the long foot of time
and hunt down the impious man.°   890
One must never, in thought and deed,
rise above the laws.
For it is a light expense to believe
that these things have power: first, the divine, whatever that
may be; and second, the laws which the long stretch of time   895
has codified forever and which are grounded in nature.°

Refrain°

What good is mere cleverness? Or rather, what god-given gifts
bring more honor to mortals
than to hold the hand of mastery
over the head of the enemy?   900
Whatever is honorable is dear always.

Epode

Happy the man° who escapes
the storm at sea and reaches harbor.
Happy, too, is he who overcomes
his toils. And in different ways one man   905
surpasses another in prosperity and power.
Besides, countless are the hopes
of countless men. Some of those hopes
end in prosperity for mortals, others vanish.

888-90: Divine justice is slow but sure.

891-96: **Reconciliation of man-made law (*nomos*) and natural law (*physis*)**: Whatever exists 'over the long ages' is not just human law (*nomos*) but natural law (*physis*) since the former is grounded in the latter. The target of this choral wisdom is Pentheus who, they imply, violates the unwritten law of worshiping the gods. But Pentheus nowhere professes atheism; he just does not see that this new god *is* a god. [Kirk 99, Leinieks 248-51].

897-901 repeat 877-81; so also 991-96 = 1011-1016. Such choral refrain, though common in Aeschylus, is unusual in Euripides; it seems designed to convey a sense of order, solemnity, and ritual to the song.

902-11: **'Happy the man'**: This 'pronouncement of happiness' (cp. 72n.) gradually builds to an impressive climax: Happy is he who a) escapes danger; b) overcomes toils; c) prospers materially; d) nourishes hopes. But most blessed is he who e) enjoys happiness in the here and now of daily life.

But I count him blessed whose life,   910
from day to day, is happy.°

ACT IV°

[Enter the Stranger from the palace] °

The Stranger
You there — the one eager to see what you ought not to see°
and seeking things not to be sought, I mean you Pentheus —
come out in front of the house. Be seen by me
wearing your costume of a woman, a maenad, a bacchant,°   915
spying on your mother and her troop.

[Enter Pentheus from the palace; his new costume resembles the Stranger's.]
Well, you look very much like one of Cadmus' daughters.°

Pentheus
And truly I seem to myself to see two suns°

911: **What constitutes happiness?** The word 'happy' (repeated at 902, 904, 911)
translates *eudaimôn* (see Glossary, 'Happiness'). In this stanza "*eudaimôn* does
not mean the hedonism of transient pleasures but the *permanent* happiness
brought by [Dionysiac] initiation to every day, in contrast to the illusory hopes
for wealth and power." [Seaford 1994, 404]

Act IV, mirror of Act II: In Act II (434-518 = 85 lines) the Stranger (physically bound) is
ushered in and out by Pentheus. Act IV (912-76 = 65 lines) reverses the situation of
Act II; now Pentheus (mentally bound) is ushered in and out by the Stranger. Act
IV can be divided structurally according to the several manifestations of Pentheus'
delusion, moving from the physical (the changed perceptions of his eyes) to the
psychological (the changed perceptions of his mind). Dodds (192) comments: "The
scene between these two is as gruesome as anything in literature."

912: Why does Dionysus enter before Pentheus? "It is dramatically more effective
but also because he is acting as his mystagogue," i.e. his initiator into the
Dionysiac mysteries. (Seaford 1996, 223)

912: **Pentheus as 'Peeping Tom'?** To describe him as such (Dodds xliii) is to suggest
that his behavior is sexually perverted. That seems too strong. See Glossary,
'Pentheus as Peeping Tom.'

915: **The physical resemblance between the Stranger and Pentheus.** Both have
long hair (235, 455, 493; 831), both look like maenads (491; 835-36, 915), and
both carry a thyrsus (495; 835, 941). All of which means that Pentheus looks
like his mother too.

917: **Clothes and power:** Pentheus' act of disrobing divests him not only of his
regalia but symbolizes the physical dissolution of his kingship and the psychological dissolution of his identity. Similarly when Agamemnon takes off
his boots to walk on the blood-red tapestry laid down by Clytemnestra, he
symbolically divests himself of his kingship and power; his murder follows
quickly. (*Agamemnon* 905-11, 944-49)

918: Euripides' influence on Virgil: A striking passage in the *Aeneid* (4.469-70) alludes to these lines. Dido, the queen of Carthage, in a nightmarish frenzy at
being rejected by Aeneas, is described thus: "Just like Pentheus in his madness sees oncoming troops of Furies, and sees twin suns and a twofold Thebes
display themselves to the view." (Cp. also *Aeneid* 4.300-33, 7. 385-405)

and a double Thebes, that fortress of seven mouths.°
And you seem to be a bull leading us in front   920
and horns seem to have sprouted on your head.
But *were* you a beast before? Because certainly you are a bull now.°

The Stranger
The god accompanies me. Although initially ill-disposed
he is in alliance with us. So now, at last, you see what you ought to
see.°

Pentheus
How do I look, then? Don't I carry myself like Ino   925
or like Agave, my mother?°

The Stranger
Seeing you I seem to see those very women.
But this braid of hair here is out of place,
not as I had arranged it under your headband.

Pentheus
While I was inside the palace I shook my head forward   930
and shook it back, revelling like a bacchant, and jostled it out of
place.°

The Stranger
Well, we'll set it back in place since it is our concern
to serve you. Now, then, straighten up your head.

Pentheus
There — you fix it since I give myself up to you.°

918-19: **Two suns and two cities:** On this surrealistic scene, see Glossary 'Pentheus'
double vision.'
920-22: **Dionysus as a bull**: How is it that Pentheus sees Dionysus as a bull? And
does he see the Stranger as well? See Glossary, 'Pentheus' vision of Dionysus
as a bull.'
924: An allusion to 502 where the Stranger told Pentheus that his impiety prevented
his *seeing* Dionysus.
925-44: **Transvestite scene as *meta-theater*** (i.e. theater conscious of itself as theater). The costume items mentioned at 830-36 (dress, headband, fawnskin,
thyrsus) are now, in this tragically comic scene, being proudly worn by
Pentheus as instructed by his fashion designer. Wolff (1982, 263) notes that
Dionysus "plays the part, within his play, of the play's director making back-
stage preparations and conducting a rehearsal. The theatrical process itself...
has become part ot the play's subject. This is a mark of a late, self-conscious
stage in the history of an art form."
930-33: These lines reverse the situation of 492-94 where it was Dionysus' hair that
was the center of attention.
934: Although Pentheus intends his words "I give myself up to you" to mean "I
depend on your will," the Greek also suggests an ominous irony, namely "I
dedicate myself to you as a religious offering."

The Stranger

Your girdle, too, is loose and the pleats of your dress   935
hang crooked below your ankles.

Pentheus

Yes, at least around the right foot they do indeed seem out of order.

[Checking over his shoulder at the situation in the rear.]
But on the left side my dress holds straight along the heel.°

The Stranger

Surely you will consider me the first of your friends
when, contrary to expectation, you see the Bacchae chaste and sober.
   940

Pentheus

Will I look more like a bacchant if I hold the thyrsus
in my right hand or here, in my left?

The Stranger

You must lift it in your right hand to keep time with the right foot.
I congratulate you that you've changed your mind.

Pentheus

Could I carry the glens of Mt. Cithaeron,   945
Bacchae and all, on my shoulders?

The Stranger

You could if you wanted. Before you had a mind that was unhealthy
but now you have just the one you need.

Pentheus

Shall we bring levers? Or should I tear the glens up with my own two
   hands,
jacking the peaks up with my shoulders or arms?   950

The Stranger

No, please don't destroy the shrines of the Nymphs
and the haunts of Pan where he plays his pipes.

Pentheus

Good point. Our victory over the women must come not by strength.
I'll hide my body among the fir trees.

The Stranger

You will be hidden in a hiding place perfect for hiding!°   955

937-38: **Tragic comedy.** The sight of the maenads' arch-enemy, himself dressed as a
   maenad intently adjusting his feminine costume, has a genuine comic element. See Glossary, 'Pentheus as tragic comedian.'
955: The repetition "hidden...hiding...hiding" highlights the secretive nature of
   Pentheus' activity and foreshadows the ominous events that will happen at
   this 'hiding' place.

From there you can do your crafty spying on the maenads.

Pentheus

Yes indeed. Like birds in a bush, I reckon they are in the thickets
held fast in the sweetest snares of love-making.°

The Stranger

Isn't this the very thing you're being sent to guard against?
You will catch them perhaps unless you are caught first.   960

Pentheus

Escort me through the main streets of Thebes.
For I am the only man of all the Thebans to dare this.°

The Stranger

Indeed you are the only one who toils for this city, the only one!°
Therefore the contests you deserve await you.°
So follow me. I will go as the escort who brings you salvation°   965
but another will lead you back from there.°

Pentheus

Yes, my mother.

The Stranger

You will be conspicuous to all.°

Pentheus

For this very reason I am going.

The Stranger

You will be *carried* home.

Pentheus

You mean in the lap of luxury.°

958: Pentheus again returns to his notion of the maenads as obsessed with sex (cp. 223).

962: **Pentheus' manhood:** He has overcome his earlier shame (840) of taking Thebes' *back* streets. "Ironically, it is in female dress that Pentheus boasts of his male bravery." (Seaford 1996, 226)

963: **Pentheus as the lonely scapegoat:** The ambiguity of 963 ('toils' could also mean 'suffers') foreshadows the dying Pentheus as a scapegoat (*pharmakos*) whose death will purify Thebes' collective guilt. For parallels between the fates of Pentheus and Jesus, see Glossary, 'Pentheus as scapegoat.'

964: The Greek noun for 'contest' is *agôn* (again at 975, 1163); it can also mean 'ordeal' in the sense of 'agon-y' but Pentheus is oblivious to the Stranger's conscious ambiguity.

964-65: **The ritual pattern behind Pentheus' death:** see Glossary, 'Pentheus' death.'

966-70: The long dialogue (923-65) between the Stranger and Pentheus switches now at its climax from alternating couplets to alternating half-lines (called *antilabe*; see 189n). The emphatic breaking of the five climatic verses of this act (966-70) at their metrical mid-points intensifies the irony of the swift exchange.

967: Pentheus will indeed be conspicuous. See 1139-43.

968: Pentheus proudly imagines he will be carried home in a chariot.

The Stranger
You will indeed be in your mother's arms.

Pentheus
You'll actually force me to be broken by pampering!

The Stranger
And *what* a pampering it will be! 970

Pentheus
I am taking hold of what I deserve.

The Stranger
You are wondrous, wondrous and you are going to wondrous suffer-
ings°
so that you will find your fame towering as high as heaven.

[Turning toward distant Cithaeron to address the Bacchae there]
Stretch out your hands, Agave, and you, her sisters,
daughters of Cadmus. I am leading this young man here°
into a great contest and the victor will be myself and Bromios.° 975
The event itself will show the rest.°

[The Stranger escorts Pentheus off, stage left, towards Cithaeron]

Chorus of Asian Bacchae°
Strophe 1
Go forth, swift hounds of Frenzy,° go to the mountain
where the daughters of Cadmus convene their congregation.
Sting them with frenzy
against the man in his woman-miming costume, 980

971: The triple repetition is again (as at 955 and 962-63) ominous. The adjective
'wondrous' (*deinos*) can also mean 'disastrous.' Pentheus, of course, is oblivious to the Stranger's irony.

974: "It is apt that Pentheus is called a 'young man' in the context of his child-like
devotion to his mother: cp. 1118, 1121, 1174, 1185. In vase-painting he is generally beardless." (Seaford 1996, 227)

975: **The distinction between the Stranger and Dionysus is dissolved here.** The
expression 'the victor will be' is emphatically singular and so points to just
one victor. This indicates that "the fiction that the Stranger and Dionysus are
different entities, which they still were at line 849, has finally been given up."
(Rijksbaron 123; Seaford 1996, 227).

976: **"The tying of the plot is now complete, the untying about to begin."** (Dodds
197) See Aristotle *Poetics* 1455 b24-32.

FIFTH CHORAL SONG (977-1023): Inspired by the Stranger's preceding words,
this excited song of revenge covers an imagined interval of many hours—the
time needed for the disastrous offstage action to transpire (i.e. Pentheus' ten
mile trip to Cithaeron, his death, and the messenger's return to Thebes).

977: **The goddess Frenzy (*Lyssa*):** The chorus here picks up the Stranger's injunc-
tion to them at 851 about frenzy (*lyssa*). The goddess 'Frenzy' has powers
similar to the Furies (*Erinyes*). Like them, she is a daughter of Night who
causes frenzy and hunts with hounds.

the deluded spy of the maenads.
First his mother, unseen, from a smooth rock
will see him playing the spy
and call out to the maenads:°
    "O Bacchae, who is this searcher   985
    of the mountain-running daughters of Cadmus
    who has come, has come to the mountain, to the mountain?
    Who gave him birth? For he was not born
    from the blood of women. No, his birth was from some lioness
    or from the Libyan Gorgons." °   990

Refrain
  Let justice go openly!
  Let sword-bearing justice go forth,
  slaying him
  right through the throat —
  the godless, lawless, unjust,   995
  earth-born offspring of Echion.

Antistrophe 1
  Since he, with unjust thought and unlawful rage
  concerning your secret rites, Bacchus,
  and those of your mother,
  sets forth with a maddened mind and insane purpose   1000
  believing he will overpower by force the unconquerable,
  that is to say, sensible judgment.
  But death is unhesitating where divine things are concerned°
  and to behave as a mortal entails a life free of pain.
    I do not begrudge cleverness. But I rejoice   1005
    in hunting down these other things that are great and manifest°
    — for they lead a man's life towards the good —
    namely to be pure and reverent throughout the day and

985-90: The chorus' point: inhuman conduct implies inhuman origin. But there is unconscious irony here; it was Agave who gave birth to Pentheus and who will think his head is that of a young lion; cp. 1141-42 (Dodds 201, Kirk 107).

990: Gorgons: three monstrous sisters with snakes in their hair (like the Bacchae). Their gaze turned any lookers to stone. Medusa, the most famous Gorgon, suffered a fate similar to Pentheus, i. e. decapitation.

1003: "False judgments about the gods are punished by death, and death accepts no excuses." (Kirk 108)

1005-6: The text here (and elsewhere at 1002-07) is uncertain. The gist is: "'I do not grudge (anybody, e.g. Pentheus, his) cleverness (seeing that he will derive no joy from it); but my joy is in pursuing....' The chorus, who believe that *to sophon* ('cleverness') should be avoided, can confidently say that if there are people who are nonetheless foolish enough to covet it they are quite free to do so. Of such people the gods will take care, as they have emphatically proclaimed in the preceding lines." (Rijksbaron 129-30).

into the night and, by rejecting customs
outside the sphere of justice, to honor the gods.   1010
Refrain
Let justice go openly!
Let sword-bearing justice go forth,
slaying him
right through the throat —
the godless, lawless, unjust,   1015
earth-born offspring of Echion.
Epode
Appear as a bull
or a many-headed snake
or a fire-blazing lion to behold.
Go, Bacchus, beast, and with a laughing face   1020
cast the noose of death
on the hunter of the Bacchae
as he falls under the herd of maenads.°

ACT V°

[Enter Messenger #2, stage left; he is Pentheus' personal attendant,]
Messenger #2
O house, you that once were fortunate throughout Greece,
[house of the old man from Sidon° who sowed in the soil   1025
the earth-born crop of the serpent-dragon]
how I lament for you!
Though I am only a slave, still I lament.
Chorus-leader
What is the matter? Have you some news to reveal from the Bacchae?
Messenger
Pentheus is dead — the son of Echion, his father.   1030
Chorus-leader *[singing]* °
O lord Bromios, you have revealed yourself a mighty god!

1021-23 present textual and interpretive problems. Another possible translation is:
"... cast a noose on the hunter of the Bacchae when he has *fallen* beneath the
murderous herd of maenads."

Act V (1024-1152) has two sections: a) 1024-1042 = lyric dialogue #2 = announcement of, and choral reaction to, Pentheus' death; b) 1043-1152 = narrative
description of Pentheus' death at hands of Bacchae.

1025-26 [possibly interpolated]: The old man from Sidon, capital of Phoenicia, is
Cadmus (cp. 171n.).

1031-42: The chorus-leader *sings* her lines from the orchestra as the messenger *speaks*
his (iambic) lines from the stage. She sings in an excited meter that emphasizes
her joy at the news of Pentheus' death.

Messenger
What do you mean? Why do you say this? Do you truly rejoice,
woman, in the misfortunes of one who was my master?

Chorus-leader
I am a foreigner. I cry "euoi" in ecstasy with my barbarian songs.
No longer do I cower under the fear of chains.   1035

Messenger
Do you deem Thebes so devoid of men
[that you will go unpunished for rejoicing in Pentheus' death].°

Chorus-leader
Dionysus, it is Dionysus, not Thebes
who has power over me.

Messenger
That, indeed, is pardonable but it is not honorable, women,
to rejoice at the evils that have been done.   1040

Chorus-leader
Tell me, speak! By what doom did he die,
the unjust man, contriver of unjust deeds?

Messenger°
When we had left behind the last settlements of this Theban land
and gone beyond the streams of Asopus°
we were striking into the hill country of Cithaeron°   1045
both Pentheus and I, for I was following my master
and the stranger who was our escort for the viewing.°
    First, then, we stop and sit in a grassy glen
silencing the sounds of our feet and tongues

1037: Bracketed because it is missing from the Greek text. Context allows us to fill
    in the meaning.
1043-1152: **SECOND MESSENGER SPEECH** (110 lines): In the first messenger
    speech (677-774) a herdsman (714) had described the miracles of the Theban
    Bacchae on Mt. Cithaeron, including the tearing apart (*sparagmos*) of bulls. In
    the present speech one of Pentheus' slaves (1028, 1046), who was apparently
    on stage with Pentheus earlier (cp. 1043-47) and departed with him and the
    Stranger at 965-76, describes the tearing apart of his master.
1044: The Asopus River separated Thebes from Mt. Cithaeron (cp. 750n.).
1043-45: The movement of the male trio here from *city* across *river* to *mountain*
    reverses the earlier movement of the trio of sisters with their maenads from
    mountain across *river* to the *villages*. The routing of the male villagers then
    (761-64) foreshadowed the routing of Pentheus here (1111-12).
1047: **Pentheus as Olympic victor:** The messenger refers to the Cithairon mission
    as a *theôria* ('a viewing'), i.e. a sending of state ambassadors to the games. In
    this part of the play Pentheus is thought of as Thebes' champion competitor
    (963), her ace horse jockey (1074, 1108) who is going to a contest (*agôn*, 964) to
    achieve fame (*kleos*, 972). But Dionysus, his official escort (*pompos*, 965, 1047),
    will end up as 'the triumphant victor' (1146). (Leinieks 172-75)

so as to see but not be seen.° 1050
There was a hollow, surrounded by high cliffs,
watered by streams, thickly shaded by pines.
In that very spot the maenads sat plying their hands in tasks of delight.°
For some of them were crowning anew their worn-out thyrsi
making them long-haired with ivy. 1055
Others, like fillies set free from their painted yokes,
were singing bacchic songs to one another.
But the wretched Pentheus, not seeing the mob of women,
spoke the following words:
    "Stranger, from where we stand
    my eyes cannot discern the maenads in their sick frenzy. 1060
    But on the banks of the ravine, by climbing a high-necked fir,
    I could see more clearly the shameful deeds of the maenads."°
Just then I see miraculous deeds from the stranger.
Seizing hold of the sky-high branch of a fir tree
he kept tugging, tugging, tugging it down to the black ground.° 1065
The fir was arched like a bow being strung
or like a bulging wheel being chiselled on a revolving lathe.
In this way the stranger, tugging on this mountain branch
with both hands, was bending it to the earth, doing deeds not mortal.
And seating Pentheus on the fir's branches 1070
he lets the sapling go straight up through his hands
without shaking it, taking care not to throw the rider.
High up into the high sky the fir towered,°
my master saddled on its back.°

1050: This messenger, like the first one, emphasizes three times (1050, 1063, 1077)
that he was an eye-witness to the events he is reporting.

1051-53: This secluded, cliff-bound glen seems charming enough with its water,
shade, and trees. But all these features of the traditional *locus amoenus* ('de-
lightful place') soon become witnesses of the ritual sacrifice and murder.

1059-62: This direct quotation of Pentheus' words is the first of four direct quotations in this second messenger speech (cp. Dionysus at 1079-81, Agave at
1106-9, 1118-21). There were two quotations in the first messenger speech:
the city-slicker at 718-21 and Agave at 731-33. One effect of such quotations is
to draw the spectator more directly into the sphere of the actions described.

1065: 'tugging, tugging, tugging': "The threefold repetition, unique in tragic dialogue, suggests the slow descent of the tree-top." (Dodds 210)

1073: Dionysus' prophecy that Pentheus would find his fame *rising to the sky* (972)
has now come true!

1074: **Fir tree as phallic symbol of Dionysus:** "The fir tree has become a thyrsus
with Pentheus in maenadic attire crowning its tip as the ivy does the narthex
[fennel stalk].... Dionysus has manifested himself in this enormous symbol
of his power, the tree-thyrsus.... The scene may represent an erection, not of
Pentheus, but of the god himself and therefore a manifestation of his power,
just as phalli are raised in the Dionysiac procession as symbols of his power
of fertility." (Kalke 416-17)

But rather than seeing the maenads from above he was seen by them.
For he was just becoming visible on his lofty perch   1076
when the stranger completely vanished from sight
and some voice from the air— I would guess Dionysus' —
shouted out:
    "Young women, I bring him
    who made you and me and my holy rites   1080
    a laughing-stock. But take revenge on him!"
And while it was speaking these words
a light of holy fire was towering up between heaven and earth.°
    The high air fell silent, and silent, too, were the leaves
of the forest meadow; nor could you hear the cry of beasts.   1085
Not hearing the voice clearly with their ears
the women bolted straight up and cast their heads about.
Again he commanded them. And when the daughters of Cadmus
recognized clearly the command of Bacchus they darted forth
with the speed of a dove [their swift feet impetuously
    carrying them —   1090
his mother Agave and her kindred sisters] and all the Bacchae.
They were leaping through the valleys
swollen by winter torrents and over jagged cliffs,
frenzied by the god's breath.°
But when they saw my master sitting on the fir tree   1095
first they kept hurling hard-hitting stones at him,°
climbing upon a rock that towered on the opposite ravine
and he was bombarded by their javelins of fir.
Others sent their thyrsi through the air at Pentheus.

1083: **Dionysus as god of lightning** (cp. 595): The fire stretching from earth to heaven
    seems to be continuous flash of lightning, yet another way Dionysus speaks
    to his worshipers. (Leinieks 100)

1078-90: **Sophocles as imitator of Euripides?** "This impressive passage is worth
    comparing with the almost contemporary lines in which the 90 year old
    Sophocles described the supernatural summons to Oedipus, *Oedipus at Colonus*
    1621-9." (Dodds 212) Perhaps Sophocles, while writing *Oedipus at Colonus*,
    saw a copy of the *Bacchae* before its production.

1094: **The god's breath:** Dionysus breathes upon the soul of each member in the
    cult group and thereby controls them; thus each "becomes part of the cult
    group (*thiasos*) in his soul (*psyche*)" (75). "The divine breathing upon not only
    results in divine control of the human subject, but it also makes the human
    subject divinely empowered (*en-theos*).... That does not mean that one has a
    god within him, but rather that one has within him power originating from a
    god." (Leinieks 92-97, citing several sources about gods 'breathing upon'
    human subjects, e.g. Euripides *Phoenician Women* 789-94, Plato *Ion* 533d-e).

1096: Earlier in the play (356-57), Pentheus had imagined that Dionysus would be
    brought to justice by being stoned to death at Pentheus' command. Now the
    tables have turned.

Theirs was a cruel targetting but they missed the mark.° 1100
For the poor wretch sat too high, beyond the reach
of their zeal, though still captive to helplessness.
Finally, blasting some branches of oak with the force of a thunderbolt,°
the Bacchae set about tearing up the tree's roots with these unforged
    levers.°
But when they failed to accomplish the goals of their toiling 1105
Agave spoke:
    "Come, stand round in a circle, maenads,
    and let each of us take hold of a branch
    so we can capture the mounted beast °
    lest he report the god's secret dances."°
And the women put a thousand hands to the fir tree and tore it 1110
out of the earth. High up Pentheus sat and from that height
he falls, crashing to the ground with a thousand wailing cries.°
He understood that he was near evil.
It was his own mother who first, as sacred priestess, began the
    slaughter°
and falls upon him. He threw the headband from his hair 1115
hoping that the wretched Agave, recognizing her son, might not kill him.
Touching her cheek, he spoke:
    "It is I, mother, your son

1096-1100: **Pentheus as scapegoat.** "The pelting of Pentheus corresponds...to the
    pelting of the victim with barley groats. The collective violence that in the
    normal sacrificial pelting is symbolic has against Pentheus become real, with
    the result that he resembles the *pharmakos* (scapegoat) pelted with stones."
    (Seaford 1996, 236). See Glossary, 'Pentheus as scapegoat.'
1103: Just as Semele was blasted by Zeus' thunderbolt (6), so Pentheus will be by
    the thunder-force of the maenads. The rare verb used here ('to blast utterly
    with thunder') belonged to the special vocabulary of Dionysiac cult.
1104: The attempt at 'tearing up' (*sparagmos*) the trees here foreshadows the immi-
    nent *sparagmos* of Pentheus (1127, 1135, 1220). See Glossary, 'Tearing-to-pieces.'
1108: **First indication of Agave's delusion about her son:** At 1215 and 1278 the
    'beast' of 1108 becomes further defined as a 'lion' (cp. chorus at 989-90).
1109: Agave's notion of 'secret dances' reminds us that Pentheus is being punished
    because he has, without being initiated successfully in the god's religious
    mysteries, invaded a sacred site and a sacred rite.
1110-12: **Dionysus as god of trees:** The ancient traveller Pausanias (2nd c. A.D.)
    saw at Corinth two gold-covered wooden statues of Dionysus ('Loosener'
    and 'Reveller') said to have been made from the tree on which Pentheus sat.
    The Corinthians had been ordered by the Delphic oracle "to discover the tree
    and worship it equally with the god. So they made the tree into these im-
    ages." (2.2.7). As Dodds (209) notes, "This suggests that the tree [on which
    Pentheus sat] is no less an agent and embodiment of Dionysus than the
    Stranger who vanishes as soon as the tree comes into action (1076 f)."
1114: Agave's Dionysian sacrifice is the first climax of the messenger's speech (cp.
    1141); on her perversion of sacrifice see Glossary, 'Sacrifice.'

Pentheus to whom you gave birth in the house of Echion.
Take pity, mother, and do not,   1120
because of my errors,° kill your son."
But Agave, foaming at the mouth and rolling her protruding eyeballs,°
not thinking what she ought to think,
was held fast by the Bacchic god nor was Pentheus persuading her.
Seizing his left arm with her forearms   1125
and pressing her foot against the doomed man's ribs
she tore off his shoulder,° not by her own strength —
no, the god gave a special ease to her hands.°
Ino completed the job, tearing off his other shoulder,
ripping pieces of flesh while Autonoe and the entire mob of Bacchae 1130
continued to press upon him. Every kind of shout was mingled together,
and for as long as he had breath he screamed in pain
while the maenads were crying out in triumph. One was carrying an arm,
another a foot still in its hunting boot. The ribs were laid bare
by the tearing apart. All the women, with blood-spattered hands,   1135
were playing ball with Pentheus' flesh.°
His body lies scattered, one part beneath rugged rocks,
another in the thick foliage of the forest,
not easily sought out. But the pitiful head, the very one
which his mother just then happened to take with her hands,   1140
she impales on the tip of her thyrsus and carries it,°

1121: **Pentheus' recognition of the truth?** For the first time he confesses to 'errors'
    but what he means, beyond the fact of his physical danger, is unclear. See
    Glossary, 'Pentheus' moment of truth.'
1122: **Agave's foaming mouth and protruding eyeballs**: Well-known symptoms of
    abnormal mental states and, in particular, of epilepsy. Mother becomes like
    son to the degree that she confuses 'what she ought to think' just as Pentheus
    had confused 'what he ought to see' (924).
1125-27: Pentheus' death in art: "Of the second messenger's speech, only the ultimate
    destruction of Pentheus has parallels in Attic art. The earliest depictions appear
    on three vases before the end of the sixth century, a century before Euripides'
    Bacchae and several decades before Aeschylus' *Pentheus*." (Carpenter 116; cp.
    Dodds 217: "This moment is often represented in ancient works of art.")
1128: Agave's amazing strength: the last sinister manifestation of Dionysiac effort-
    lessness. (Dodds 218)
1136: A macabre ball-game: "Some members of Euripides' audience must have dis-
    cerned in this a ghastly contrast with the game of ball played by Nausicaa
    and her handmaidens in *Odyssey* 6.100—a slight, but probably intended, *arrière
    pensée* [secondary intention]." (Stanford 179)
1141: **Impaling of Pentheus' head**: The second climax of this speech, even more har-
    rowing than the first (cp. 1114). "Euripides creates a Pentheus who is transformed
    visually into a symbol of Dionysus. Pentheus becomes the thyrsus of the god:
    first he is crowned with long hair and a *mitra* [headband], then he himself crowns
    the tip of a fir tree raised by the maenads on the mountain, and finally he be-
    comes the literal crown of the thyrsus carried by his mother." (Kalke 410)

as if it were the head of a mountain lion,° through the middle of
   Cithaeron,
leaving behind her sisters in the choruses of dancing maenads.°
Rejoicing in her ill-fated prey she comes inside these city walls
calling upon the Bacchic god as her "fellow huntsman,"   1145
her "comrade in the chase," the "triumphant victor"
in whose honor she carries off tears as a victory-prize.
   So I will depart out of the way of this disaster
before Agave returns to the palace.
Moderation and reverence for things divine,   1150
this is the best course. And it is also, I think,
the wisest possession for those mortals who use it.°

[Exit Messenger #2, stage right]

Chorus of Asian Bacchae°
Let us lift up our feet and dance for Bacchus!
Let us lift up our voices and shout for the doom of Pentheus,
descendant of the serpent.   1155
He took the clothes of a woman
and the fennel-rod fashioned into a beautiful thyrsus,
a sure warranty of death in Hades,°

1142: **Pentheus' head as that of a lion** (another one of Dionysus' animal manifestations): Such is Agave's consistent perception: 1196, 1215, 1278; cp. 1142, 1183,
   1210, 1237.
1143: "Agave's separation from the other maenads seems connected with her leading
   role in the kill (1114, 1183, 1239). Its dramatic function is to allow her pathetic
   entry to be isolated." (Seaford 1996, 239)
1150-52: **Moral of messenger's story:** "Moderation and piety toward the gods
   are man's wisest possessions." This traditional but powerful platitude (cp.
   Antigone 1348-50 on Creon's tragic fate) restates the answer to the crucial
   question asked by the chorus twice earlier (877-81 = 897-901) about the nature
   of wisdom. (Dodds 219)
SIXTH CHORAL ODE (1153-64): A celebration of Pentheus' death and Agave's
   homecoming, as if she was a victor returning from the Olympic games (1160).
   It is the play's only astrophic ode (a single stanza with no metrically responding counterpart) and is sung in an excited meter. This last ode is the play's
   shortest because "as the action hurries to its climax there is time only for a
   brief song of triumph.... The opening words suggest a joyful accompanying
   dance; but as the thoughts of the singers turn from Pentheus to Agave horror,
   if not pity, creeps in. The last lines prepare the audience for what their eyes
   must now meet." (Dodds 219; cp. Leinieks 278)
1156-58: **Hades and Dionysus:** By dressing like the maenads and taking up their
   main instrument, the thyrsus, Pentheus assured his own death (cp. 857-59,
   1141). The irony, then, is that what should have been Pentheus' means of
   initiation into Dionysus' cult group has become instead his means of initiation into Hades' house. Hence the apparent opposites, Hades (death) and
   Dionysus (exuberant life) turn out to be one and the same (cp. Heraclitus
   fragment 22 B 15 DK).

having a bull as his leader to doom.°
Cadmean Bacchae, you have made your victory hymn renowned, 1160
but it ends in a dirge of wailing, of tears.
A fine contest — to plunge your hands
in the blood of your child so that they drip with his blood!

EXODOS°
Chorus-leader (*interrupting the song, addressing her companions*)
Stop! I see Pentheus' mother, Agave,   1165
rushing toward the house, her eyes rolling wildly.
Receive this reveler of the god of ecstasy!

[*Enter Agave alone, stage left, excitedly dancing (cp. 1230-31) in her maenad costume; she carries Pentheus' blood-stained head (i. e. mask) atop her thyrsus.*]

Lyric Dialogue°
Strophe 1
Agave
Asian Bacchae...

Chorus-leader
                    Why do you call out on me, woman?

Agave
We bring from the mountains to the palace
a freshly cut tendril,   1170
a blessed prey!

Chorus-leader
I see it and will accept you as a fellow-reveller.

Agave
I captured him without any snares,
this young whelp [of a mountain lion],

1159: The chorus is referring to Pentheus' vision of Dionysus as a bull at 920-22 (cp. 100, 1017).
EXODOS ('a going out,' with reference to the chorus' departure, as at the end of most Greek tragedies). This epilogue presents the play's tragic 'reversal' which Aristotle defined as "a change of the action to its opposite...which must conform to probability or necessity." (*Poetics* 1452a 22-24). That reversal had been foreshadowed at 1147 where the messenger told 'she who carried off tears as a victory-prize.'
1168-99: **Lyric Dialogue #3:** (cp. 576-603, 1024-42). The singing here continues the swift and excited choreography of the preceding song. There are two stanzas which respond to one another metrically: *strophe* (1168-83): chorus asks Agave about her hunting of a lion cub (= Pentheus) on Cithaeron; *antistrophe* (1184-99): Agave, in her frenzy, invites the chorus to share in a feast of her 'catch.'
1169-71: Life imitates art. Agave's carrying of Pentheus' head here inspired the real life decapitation of the Roman general Crassus 350 years later. Cp. Plutarch *Life of Crassus* (33) and Leinieks 310-11.

as you can see for yourself. 1175
Chorus-leader
Where in the wilderness did you capture him?
Agave
Cithaeron...
Chorus-leader
                Cithaeron?
Agave
                        ...slaughtered him.
Chorus-leader
Who was the woman who struck him?
Agave
                                First honors belong to me.
"Blessed Agave" is what the worshippers call me.° 1180
Chorus-leader
Who else struck him?
Agave
                Cadmus'...
Chorus-leader
Cadmus' what?
Agave
                His daughters,
but only after me. Only after me did they lay their hands
on this beast here. Lucky indeed is this catch!°
Antistrophe 1
Agave [*gently caressing Pentheus' head*]
Share in the feast, then.
Chorus-leader
                What? Am I to share in this, wretched woman?°

1180: One of the play's most bitter ironies—that Agave should call herself 'blessed'
(*makar*) when she is carrying the head of Pentheus whose name ('Man of Pain')
means the exact opposite of 'blessed.'

1181-83: **Agave as victor in a ritual competition:** As such, she "enjoys some es-
pecial status in the *thiasos* (cult group): she is 'the priestess of the slaughter'
(1114)—hence, apparently her extraordinary exaltation." (Dodds 224).

1184: **Agave as cannibal:** She still thinks Pentheus' head is the head of a lion, hence
she suggests feasting on it. The idea of eating Pentheus' remains raw (= *omo-
phagia*, see 135-39n.) repels even Dionysus' most ardent worshippers. Animals
might eat humans, as did Actaeon's dogs (see 337-41n.), but humans eating
humans goes beyond the pale. Agave, in her delusion, ignores their reaction
of pity (cp. 1200-1). She will reiterate her invitation to Cadmus at 1242 and
will receive a similar response.

Agave
The bull is still young:°   1185
beneath his crest of soft hair
his cheeks are just now blooming with down.

Chorus-leader
Yes, with his mane he resembles a beast of the wild country.

Agave
The Bacchic god, being a clever hunter,
cleverly urged his maenads   1190
against this beast.

Chorus-leader
For our king is a hunter.°

Agave
Do you praise me?

Chorus-leader
                    I do praise you.

Agave
And soon the Cadmeans...

Chorus-leader
and your son Pentheus, too, ...   1195

Agave
                              will praise his mother
for capturing this lion-like prey.

Chorus-leader
So extraordinary a catch!

Agave
                    Caught in such an extraordinary way!

Chorus-leader
Do you exult in him?

Agave
                    I do indeed rejoice
since, in capturing this prey, I have accomplished
a great deed, a great deed for all to see.°

1185: **Agave's changing perception of Pentheus**: Her most consistent delusion is that he is a young lion (1142, 1196, 1215, 1278); at 1170 he seems like a shoot of ivy; here, at 1185, a young bull.

1192: **Dionysus as hunter**: There may well be a word-play here with the Greek sequence *anax agreus* ('king hunter') suggesting the name Zagreus ('great hunter'), a Cretan cult title of Dionysus. In the (Orphic) myth of Dionysus Zagreus, the Titan gods tore Dionysus apart and ate his flesh. The other gods, however, gave life to his remains and thereby resurrected him.

1199: The excited and metrically complex lyric dialogue (1168-99) that accompanied Agave's entrance now ends and the regular narrative dialogue (i. e. iambic trimeters) resumes at 1200.

Chorus-leader

Show, then, poor wretch, show to the citizens the prey   1200
that brought you victory and that now you have brought to us.°

Agave

O you dwellers of Thebes, city of beautiful ramparts,
come so you can see this prey of a beast that we,
the daughters of Cadmus, have hunted down
not with thonged Thessalian javelins,   1205
not with nets, but with the sharp white blades
of our hands. So who would brag
that he owns the weapons of spear-makers? They are useless!
With our very own hands we captured this one here
and piece by piece tore to shreds the limbs of the beast.°   1210
      Where is my father, the old man? Let him come near!
And Pentheus, my son, where is he? Let him take and raise
a sturdy ladder against the palace
so he can climb up and nail to the triglyphs°
this lion's head that I have hunted and brought here.   1215

[*Enter Cadmus, stage left, followed down the side entry ramp by a slow
procession of mute pallbearers carrying a bier with the covered remains of
Pentheus' corpse*]

Cadmus°

Follow me as you carry the sad weight of Pentheus.
Follow me, attendants, in front of the house.
I bring this body here after toiling in a thousand searches,
having found him in the folds of Cithaeron,
torn to pieces, [taking] not one limb in the same part   1220
of the ground [lying in that impenetrable forest].
      For I heard from someone the daring deeds of my daughters
just as I got back inside the city walls.

1201: This is the last of several images of Agave as an athletic victor (cp. 975, 1146-
47, 1160-63).

1209-10: **Agave's split psyche**: The word order is significant: 'the beast' (1210) is deliberately postponed so that 'this one here' (1209) can suggest Pentheus. "In a
dissociated state each 'part' of the psyche has knowledge not accessible to the
other. It is precisely *because* one part of Agave *does* know that she has murdered
Pentheus that another part does not know (rejects) it." (Devereux 38)

1214: Triglyph: a slightly projecting, three-grooved rectangular block occurring at
regular intervals in a Doric frieze; between each triglyph was a plain square
area called a metope.

1216: Cadmus' entrance answers Agave's question (1211). His final words before his
last previous exit (369) had been a warning to Pentheus lest he suffer Actaeon's
fate of being ripped apart by his own hounds (338-41). Now, ironically, Cadmus
must relate how Pentheus has been ripped apart by his own mother.

With the old man, Tiresias, I was returning from the Bacchae.°
So I bent my way back to the mountain   1225
where I recovered the child slain by the maenads.
I saw Autonoe, who once mothered Actaeon to Aristaeus,°
and Ino with her, still in the thickets,
poor wretches, and still stung with madness.
But the other, Agave, was said to be returning home   1230
with the frenzied step of a Bacchic dancer. Nor was this idle gossip
since I see her now and she is not a happy sight.

Agave [*who has, by now, taken Pentheus' head from her thyrsus and cradles it
in her arms*]

Father, now you can boast most proudly
that you, of all mortals, have sown by far the best daughters.
I mean all your daughters but especially me.   1235
For it was I who left behind the spindles at the loom
to come to greater tasks, the hunting of wild beasts with my own
    hands.°
I carry here in my arms, as you see, this prize of valor
that I captured to be hung up as a dedication
in your house. Receive it, father, in your hands!°   1240

[*Offering the head to him*]
Rejoice in the spoils I captured in the hunt!
Invite your friends to a feast! For you are blessed,
blessed by the deeds we have done!

Cadmus

[O sorrow beyond measure nor able to see.°
Murder — that's what you've done with those pitiable hands.]   1245
A fine victim is this you have struck down as a sacrifice for the gods.
And now you invite this Thebes here and me to a feast.
Alas the pain of these evils, first yours, then mine.
How the god has destroyed us — justly, yes, but too severely

1224: Earlier Cadmus had accompanied Tiresias to Mt. Cithaeron to celebrate
    Bacchus' rites (cp. 360 ff.).
1227: Aristaeus was the son of Apollo and the nymph Cyrene. The story of this
    famous bee-keeper and his pursuit of Eurydice was immortalized by Virgil
    in his fourth *Georgic*.
1236-37: Sex role reversal: Agave abandons her domestic role (as weaver; cp. 118) in
    the house (the female's normal place in Greek society) to pursue the 'greater
    task' of being a hunter in the wild.
1238-40: **Pentheus' death as an animal sacrifice:** The climax of a long series of
    details in the play's second half which suggest that Euripides saw Pentheus'
    death as following the pattern of a Greek *animal* sacrifice. For a list of aston-
    ishing parallels see Glossary, 'Pentheus' death.'
1244-45: Most editors delete these lines. For the pun on Pentheus' name *O penthos*,
    'O pain', cp. 367n.

given that lord Bromios was born within our family.° 1250

Agave

How crabbed is old age for men!
How it scowls in the eyes!
Would that my son were a skilled hunter, resembling the ways
of his mother whenever he joined the young Theban men
and aimed at the beasts! But all that boy can do 1255
is fight against the gods. He must be scolded, father, by you.
Who will call him here before me
so that he might see my blessed state?

Cadmus

Alas, alas! When you all come to your senses and realize
what you have done you will feel pain, terrible pain. 1260
But if you remain forever in your present state
you will imagine yourselves fortunate, though in reality you are most
    unfortunate.

Agave

But in all this, what is not well? What is so painful?°

Cadmus

First turn your eyes this way, up toward the sky.

Agave [*looking skyward*]

There. But why did you advise me to look at the sky? 1265

Cadmus

Does it still appear the same to you or has it undergone a change?°

Agave

It is brighter than before and more translucent.°

Cadmus

Is this fluttering sensation still in your soul?

1250: As the son of Semele, Dionysus was Cadmus' grandson.

1263-1300: **Famous 'psychotherapy scene' and its historical importance:** The alternating single line dialogue allows Cadmus, by the healing art of persuasion, to coax his daughter out of her delusion. Here we have "an important document in the history of human culture...the first surviving account of an insight-and-recall oriented psychotherapy.... Such an innovation is the natural consequence of the basic outlook of a poet who...systematically substituted psychological explanations of human motivation for traditionally supernatural ones." (Devereux 42)

1266: Cadmus begins here a barrage of questions that forces Agave herself to begin the hard labor of recalling her past; he realizes that this is the only way she will come to understand what she has done.

1267: **Cadmus as therapist:** On the mechanics of his 'treatment' of Agave see Glossary, 'Cadmus.'

Agave
I don't understand your question. But somehow...

[pausing for a moment]
somehow I am coming to my senses, changed from my previous state
of mind.°   1270

Cadmus
Could you, then, hear a question? And could you answer it clearly?

Agave
Yes, but I have completely forgotten what we just said, father.°

Cadmus
To whose house did you come when you got married?°

Agave
You gave me to Echion, one of the Spartoi, the Sown Men, as they call
them.

Cadmus
And who in this house is the son of your husband?   1275

Agave
Pentheus, by my union with his father.

Cadmus
Well then, whose face do you hold folded in your arms?°

Agave
A lion's head — at least that's what the women hunters told me.

Cadmus
Look again, straight at it. The toil of looking is brief.

1269-70: This two line interruption of the otherwise single line dialogue (1263-1300)
marks, for Agave, a decisive turn back toward reality, for both her soul (1268)
and mind (1270).

1272: Agave's amnesia: She means that she has forgotten what was said between
1216-62. Her asking Cadmus to repeat what had been said is "more than a
subterfuge permitting her to cling a little longer to the fiction of a *total* amnesia. It is also a clinically familiar, devious *request for help*, which further proves
her readiness for *insight* therapy." (Devereux 42)

1273-84: **Role of memory in Agave's recognition:** "Cadmus skillfully leads up to
the *anagnorisis* (recognition), appealing to the older memories that have not
been repressed. She remembers her husband? Her son? Then at 1277 he shoots
the crucial question at her. With averted eyes she answers 'A lion's—*or so
they told me* in the hunt.' Gently but relentlessly he forces her from this last
refuge: 'Come, you must look properly: it is only a moment's effort.' Then
she knows; but she will not or cannot speak the name until he drags it from
her. The whole dialogue is magnificently imagined." (Dodds 230)

1277: The word for 'face' here (*prosôpon*) might also mean 'mask'; it is Pentheus'
mask, of course, that Agave is carrying. The mother's dance with her son's
severed head, her ritual rejoicing over her 'bestial' victim, must have been a
shocking spectacle for Euripides' audience.

88

Agave

Ah! What do I see? What is this I am carrying in my hands?   1280

Cadmus

Look again closely so you can learn more clearly.

Agave

I see the greatest pain, wretched woman that I am.

Cadmus

Surely it doesn't resemble a lion, does it?

Agave

No. Wretch that I am, this is Pentheus' head that I am holding!°

Cadmus

Much lamented by me long before you recognized him.   1285

Agave

Who killed him? How did he come into my hands?

Cadmus

Cruel truth, how untimely is your presence!°

Agave

Speak! How my heart leaps in fear about what is coming.

Cadmus

You killed him, you and your sisters.

Agave

But where did he die? In the house? Tell me, where?   1290

Cadmus

In the very place where the hounds once tore Actaeon to pieces.°

Agave

Why did he go to Cithaeron, this doomed boy?

Cadmus

He went to mock the god and your Bacchic rites.

Agave

And in what manner did *we* get there?

Cadmus

You all were mad and the entire city was frantic with Bacchic
frenzy.   1295

1282-84: **Agave's moment of truth:** She finally realizes that the head she holds does
not belong to a lion. Her recognition induces her to begin to ask the questions,
thereby switching roles with Cadmus.

1287: The first and only time in the play that the word 'truth' (*alêtheia*) occurs.

1291: Actaeon, the son of Autonoe, was Pentheus' first cousin; see Glossary, 'Actaeon.'

Agave

Dionysus has destroyed us. Only now do I realize this.°

Cadmus

Yes, he was insulted by our insolent hybris. For you all refused to
believe he was a god.

Agave

And the most beloved body of my son, father, where is it?

Cadmus

With great difficulty I searched it out and am carrying it here.

Agave

Have all the limbs been fitted into their sockets in a decent way?   1300

Cadmus

No, not all the limbs have been reassembled; the head is still missing.°

Agave

Who is this one whom I hold in my hands as a corpse?
And how shall I, wretch that I am, tenderly
hold him to my breast? In what manner shall I sing a dirge?
Would that I might embrace every limb, son,
kissing the pieces of flesh, the very ones which I myself nourished.
In what kind of grave could I bury your body
and with what shrouds shall I cover your corpse?
And how shall I sing the native songs for you?
Come, old man, let us put back the head of the thrice-blessed boy
in a proper way and make the whole well-fitting.
Let us arrange the body as best we can.
O dearest face, o youthful cheek,
behold, with this veil I cover your head.
Your blood-stained and furrowed limbs
and parts I cover with new shrouds,
and your ribs, too, all pierced and bloody.°

1296: Agave, like Pentheus (cp. 1113, 1121), understands her error only when it is
     too late.

Text in italics: Cadmus' reply to Agave as well as most of Agave's subsequent speech
     and other portions of the dialogue in this part of the Greek manuscript are lost
     and have been reconstructed from various sources; the reconstructed portions
     are printed here in italics. For details see Appendix One.

Agave's lament over Pentheus: "The enactment of a funerary ritual at this point...moves
     the violent and disturbing action toward closure and also helps the audience
     achieve a cathartic experience of the horror they had seen. But it is, of course, a
     grotesquely intensified version of a normal ritual. Instead of a mother washing,
     laying out, and caressing the body of a son...this mourning mother actually has
     to handle and position the pieces of her son's body— a body that she herself
     dismembered. Thus this most intimate role of the mother in the last offices to a
     child here appears in this ugly and horrible form." (Segal 1994, 15-16)

Agave

    And what share had Pentheus in my folly?   1301

Cadmus

    He proved himself like all of you, showing no reverence to the god.

    Therefore the god joined everyone together in one ruin,

    all of you and Pentheus here, so as to destroy my house and me.

    And I am indeed destroyed since I was born childless, without any

        male offspring.   1305

    So now, wretched woman, I look upon this young shoot of your

        womb,

    he who has been slain so shamefully and so evilly.

    Through him the house was recovering its sight.°

    [Turning to Pentheus' corpse]°

    It was you, child, who held my palace together, you, my daughter's son,

    who were such a terror to the city. No one was willing   1310

    to commit hybris against the old man, at least not in your presence;

    for you would have exacted the proper penalty.

    But now I will be thrown out of my palace, dishonored,

    Cadmus the great who sowed the race of Thebans

    and reaped a most beautiful harvest.   1315

    O most beloved of men — for though you are dead

    still you will be counted, child, among those I love most —

    no more will you touch this chin of mine with your hand,

    no more will you call me "grandfather" as you embrace me, son —

    no more will you ask,   1320

        "Who wrongs you, old man, who dishonors you?

        Who upsets your heart and causes you pain?

        Speak up so I can punish whoever wrongs you, father."

    But now I am wretched and you are miserable

    and your mother pitiful and your sisters miserable.

    So if there is anyone who disdains the gods   1325

    let him look at the death of this man here and let him believe that gods

        exist.°

1308: Since Cadmus had no sons (1305), his grandson was the only hope for the future, his shining light.

1309-22: **Cadmus' funeral oration:** "Cadmus' lament is almost a parody of a funeral oration. It is delivered in private rather than in public and has more praise for Pentheus' domestic than civic actions.... Nor does Cadmus mention the traditional topic of fame or lasting memory." (Segal 1994, 16)

1326: **Cadmus' shattered faith:** "What once seemed to him possible matter for a 'skilful lie' (334) has proved its reality by laying his whole world in ruins." (Dodds 234) Pentheus had refused to believe any of Dionysus' series of proofs of his existence. In retribution the god has made the death of the unbeliever himself the crowning proof of his divinity.

Chorus-leader

I am pained by your fate, Cadmus. But your grandson,
he has received just punishment, though painful to you.

Agave

Father, since you see how greatly my fortunes have changed   1329
and how wretched I am who exulted proudly just moments ago,
what hands, child, will bury you?
Would that I had not taken my own pollution into my own hands!°

Cadmus

Take courage. Though the labor is painful
be assured that I will carry Pentheus' furrowed and blood-stained limbs
from this place and give them a proper burial.

[Enter Dionysus as a god atop the palace roof] °

Dionysus°

Whoever of mortals has seen these things
let him be taught very well:
Zeus is the one who sowed the god Dionysus.
In light of the deeds done,
know clearly that he is a god....

The Cadmeians spoke indecent words about me
that [Semele] was born from some mortal; all of them said this
[but Pentheus here is especially culpable.]
And it was not enough for me to be treated with hybris in these things alone
[but he himself, though a mortal, stood against us.]
He tried to chain and abuse me.
[And then, mounted on disaster, he went to the mountain
and dared to spy upon the secret rites of the maenads.]

Accordingly he died at the hands of those who least of all should have

---

Text in italics. Again, as at 1301 ff., the text has been reconstructed from various sources. The reconstructed portions are printed here in italics. Brackets indicate lines that have been made up by C. Willink for the purpose of suggesting the kind of verse that would have made sense in the particular context. For details see Appendix Two.

Dionysus' epiphany: For the first time the god appears in his divine form (*deus ex machina*, 'god out of the machine'). Earlier he was, like a Homeric god, disguised. The ancient *hypothesis* (plot summary) is our main evidence for the missing part of the god's speech: "Dionysus, having appeared, announced [initiation rituals?] to everyone. To each one he made clear what would happen in deeds so that he would not be despised in words as a man by one of those outside" [Dionysiac religion].

Dionysus' physical appearance: The actor probably did not change his mask; no firm evidence exists for mask changing. Costume changing is also not common. It would be the place of his entry (i.e. atop the palace) which would immediately signal that 'the Stranger' was now revealing himself as a god.

murdered him.
And he suffered these things [justly].
Furthermore I will not conceal the evil sufferings which the people must endure,
for you will learn that you have come upon the suffering that you deserve.
You must yield your city to foreigners after it has been sacked by the spear,
and endure many evils,
and visit many cities submitting to the yoke of slavery at the hands of the
*   Argives.*
[It is not at all necessary to exile this man in dishonor,
but as for the daughters of Cadmus, who killed him]
Ino and Agave who gave him birth
and Autonoe, the mother of Actaeon,
I say that they must leave the city, by their exile paying
the penalty for their unholy pollution of the man whom they killed
and no longer look upon their fatherland.
For it is impious for them to remain as sacrificers at the graves of the slain.

And you, wretched Agave, last of all on this day,
holding in your hands the most miserable corpse,
in your madness, Agave, you planned these things.
I save those who are pure but I hate those who dishonor me,
and as a doer of the most impious murder
your blood pollution prevents you from seeing
the day of homecoming.
What calamities you are destined to fulfill I will tell.
You, Cadmus, will be changed into a serpent and your wife,   1330
turned into a beast, will take the form of a snake, I mean Harmonia,°
Ares' daughter, whom you, though a mortal, took as your wife.
And as the oracle of Zeus says, you and your wife
will drive a wagon of oxen, leading foreigners.
You will sack many cities with your army of countless men.   1335
But when they plunder the oracle of Apollo
your foreigners will get a disastrous homecoming.
But Ares will rescue you and Harmonia
and in the land of the blessed° establish your life.°

1331: Harmonia: the idealized personification of marriage, uniting the opposite
    principles of her father and mother, namely Ares (War) and Aphrodite (Sex);
    she was the mother of Agave, Semele, Autonoe, and Ino. All the gods at-
    tended the wedding of Cadmus and Harmonia at Thebes.
1339: The land (= islands) of the blessed: a Greek version of paradise (called Elysium
    in Homer's *Odyssey*). Located at the ends of the earth, it was an Olympus-
    like place of afterlife which Zeus reserved for a very few select heroes (e. g.
    his son-in-law Menelaus; Helen; Cadmus).
1330-39: **Dionysus' predictions:** On the five main elements here and their interpre-
    tation see Glossary, 'Dionysus' bizarre predictions.'

I say these things as Dionysus, born not from a mortal father   1340
but from Zeus. If you had known how to behave wisely
when you chose otherwise, you would now be happy
and have the son of Zeus as an ally.

Cadmus
Dionysus, we beg you, we have wronged you.

Dionysus
You were late to understand us.° When you ought to have known us,
    you did not.   1345

Cadmus
We have realized our mistakes now. But your punishment is too
    severe.

Dionysus
Yes, but I am a god and was treated with hybris by you.

Cadmus
Gods ought not be like mortals in their passions.°

Dionysus
Long ago Zeus, my father, assented to these things.°

Agave
Alas, old man, it has been decreed — miserable exile.   1350

Dionysus
Why, then, do you delay what necessity mandates?
[Dionysus probably disappears from the palace roof at this point]°

1345: **Theme of late learning:** The relationship between time and knowledge is important in Greek tragedy; often, as the proverb puts it, characters only 'learn by suffering' (*Agamemnon* 177).

1348: **The passions and wrath of the gods.** "Cadmus pleads with Dionysus, as the old servant in the *Hippolytus* with Aphrodite (*Hipp.* 120)—"The gods ought to be wiser than mortals." And both plead in vain: for such gods as these the human 'ought' has no meaning. We need not conclude that the poet denies their title to worship; to do so is to confuse the Greek with the Christian conception of deity." (Dodds 238) For the thought compare Virgil *Aeneid* 1.11: "Can wrath so grievous dwell in the minds of the gods?"

1349: **Is this a weak evasion of responsibility by Dionysus?** Only "so long as we think of gods as personal agents having moral responsibility for their acts. Other Euripidean gods fall back in the same manner upon 'Destiny' or 'the Father's will' to justify their own actions and the fate of the human characters. 'The appeal to Zeus is an appeal to ultimate mystery, to a world structure in which the forces Dionysus represents are an inescapable element. With that there is no quarrelling, and Agave recognizes that this word is final.' [Winnington-Ingram]." (Dodds 238)

1351: **Does Dionysus exit now?** It seems unlikely that he would remain a silent spectator for the last 40 lines of the play. The focus now is on the two humans and their compassion toward each other.

Cadmus

O child, what a dreadful evil we have come to,
all of us — you in your misery, and your sisters,
and I in my misery. I will arrive among foreigners
as an old and alien settler. And still for me there is an oracle°   1355
that I must lead into Greece a motley army of foreigners.
Against the altars and tombs of the Greeks
I will lead Harmonia, Ares' daughter and my wife —
both of us as savage snakes — and I will lead the way
with my troop of spearmen. Nor will I have any respite from evils,° 1360
miserable man that I am, nor will I come to peace and quiet
when I sail across the downward-plunging Acheron.°

Agave [embracing Cadmus]

O father, I will go into exile and be deprived of you.

Cadmus

Why do you embrace me with your hands, wretched child,
like a swan protecting its white-haired, helpless drone of a parent? 1365

Agave

Where shall I turn after having been banished from my fatherland?

Cadmus

I do not know, child. Your father is a weak ally.

Agave°

Farewell, O palace, farewell, O city of my fathers.
I leave you in misfortune
an exile from my own bed-chambers.   1370

Cadmus

Go, then, child, to Aristaeus' [house...]

[one line is missing from the text]

Agave [slowly beginning to exit]

I mourn for you, father.

1354-62 (and 1372-80): **Did Euripides write this seemingly weak ending?** "The repetition of the oracle is lame, and 1361-2 is odd in view of 1338-9. Conceivably someone rewrote the end (as occurred in some other tragedies, e.g. *Phoenician Women, Iphigeneia at Aulis*)." [Seaford 1996, 255]

1360-62: "Cadmus finds in his eventual translation to Elysium [the land of the blessed] only a culminating cruelty. That is psychologically right: the god's mortal victims have nothing left for comfort but their mortality...and the tired old man sees himself robbed even of that." (Dodds 239)

1362: Acheron (literally = 'flowing with sorrow'): a river in northwest Greece (Thesprotia) said to have, like Lake Avernus near Naples, communication with the underworld (cp. *Odyssey* 10.513).

1368-92: The meter changes to marching anapests, an appropriate rhythm for the final departures.

Cadmus
And I mourn for you, child,
and I weep for your sisters.

Agave
For lord Dionysus has brought
this terrible brutality
into your house.

1375

Cadmus
Yes, because he suffered terribly at your hands:
his name received no honor in Thebes.°

Agave
Farewell, my father.

Cadmus
Farewell, my sorrowing daughter,
though only with difficulty could you fare well.

1380

Agave
Escort me, O friends, to where we will gather
my sisters, companions in exile and in sadness.
May I go to where
neither polluted Cithaeron [can see me]
nor I polluted Cithaeron,°

1385

nor where any memorial of the thyrsus is dedicated.
Let these — Cithaeron and the thyrsus — be the care of other Bacchae.°

*[Exit Cadmus and his attendants, stage right, carrying the bier of Pentheus;
exit Agave, stage left, into exile]°*

1378: This theme of being punished for not honoring the god is emphasized by
    Cadmus throughout the end of the play (1249, 1297, 1303, 1325-26, 1344,
    1347); but Cadmus also stresses the excessiveness of the god's punishment
    (1249, 1346, 1348).
1381: Who are Agave's 'friends'? Probably Theban women rather than the chorus
    or the attendants who carried in Pentheus' corpse at 1216. (Dodds 242)
1385: The tearing apart of Pentheus has brought pollution rather than purification;
    cp. Leinieks 167.
1387: Future maenadism at Thebes will be left to others. Agave's rejection of Dio-
    nysus and his devotees could not be more emphatic and in this final rejection
    she carries on the spirit of her son.
"**The play ends with the heavy departures, in opposite directions,** of Cadmus,
    the heroic founder of a great city, and of Agave, daughter and mother of
    kings—departures away from the palace, scene of their greatness, and off
    into the empty, friendless outside. One only has to contrast the end of *Ion*.
    We see here the dispersal of a great house, a house great enough to breed
    a god: so dangerous is it to be mortal kin to the immortals. Thus Euripides
    uses the necessary clearance of the stage to demonstrate the frailty of human
    exaltation." (Taplin 56-57)

Chorus

Many are the shapes of divinity,
many the things the gods accomplish against our expectation.
What seems probable is not brought to pass,   1390
whereas for the improbable god finds a way.
Such was the outcome of this story.°

1388-92: **Are these final five lines genuine?** Scholars are sharply divided; for the
issues of the debate see Glossary, 'Last Lines.' If they are spurious, the chorus
could have exited silently after 1387 or even after 1351, with their god
Dionysus, if (as seems probable) he exited then. [Seaford 1996, 258]

APPENDIX ONE

The lacuna after line 1300: Agave's lament

After line 1300 there are, apparently, about 30-50 verses missing. These lines must have disappeared after the twelfth century [see below], probably the result of damage to the vulnerable end portions of the medieval codex. Cadmus presumably answered Agave's question at 1300 ("Are all Pentheus' limbs fitted into their sockets in a decent way?") in some such way as "No, not all the limbs have been reassembled; the head is still missing." At this point Agave would have placed Pentheus' head, which she has been holding in her hands since at least 1233, onto the corpse on the bier and lamented his fate. Are we to imagine Agave reconstructing the corpse right on stage? Some scholars argue that such a scenario would befit the Roman dramatist Seneca but would be too crude for Euripides, especially given Greek tragedy's aversion to such graphic stagecraft. But as Dodds (218) notes on lines 1133-36 where the maenads are playing ball with Pentheus' limbs, "Euripides does not shrink from the grotesque."

There is compelling evidence [see below] from two later sources, followed by many modern scholars, that some sort of **compositio membrorum** ('reassembly of the limbs') took place on stage (cp. March 63). From a dramatic point of view such a ritual act would serve to initiate Pentheus' funeral and to provide a context for Cadmus' funeral oration (1309-22). It seems likely that this scene was the *Bacchae's* emotional climax. About the general effect of this climax Taplin (100) observes that "the object which has held our gaze in reluctant fashion for 140 lines is at last laid to rest. The point of all this business with Pentheus' head is that it is an ambivalent object which sums up a central ambivalence in the play...On the one hand the head may be seen [as] the trophy of a great hunt, a triumph... [on the other hand] the pollution of kin-murder, exile, the end of the royal line."

Despite the gaps in the *Bacchae* manuscripts we can get an idea of Agave's speech from two later sources. First is the general account of the rhetorician Apsines (of Gadara in Phoenicia) who taught at Athens about A.D. 235. I quote from his *Art of Rhetoric* 401-402: "Another way we will arouse pity is to blame ourselves. It is possible to find this in the tragic poets. In Euripides, for instance, Pentheus' mother Agave, after being set free from her madness and recognizing that her own son has been torn to pieces, accuses herself and arouses pity." And more tellingly with regard to the staging of the *Bacchae* Apsines writes: "Euripides employed this method when he wanted to arouse pity for Pentheus. For his mother, holding each one of his limbs in her hands, laments them one at a time."

A second source for Agave's lament is the host of fragments from a cento (9th-12th century A.D.) known as the *Christus Patiens* or *"The Sufferings of Christ,"* a patchwork religious drama of 2,610 verses assigned by the manuscripts to Gregorios of Nazianos (4th century A.D.) but attributed by most scholars to an unskilled Byzantine author (possibly Constantine Manasses) who had at his disposal an undamaged text of the *Bacchae*. [The definitive edition of the *Christus Patiens* is by Andre Tuilier *Grégoire De Naziane: La passion Du Christ: Tragédie* Paris 1969.] The play contains a large number of (modified) verses from seven Euripidean tragedies (about 200 from the *Bacchae* alone) as well as a few from Aeschylus and Lycophron. I have translated in the body of my text those fragments that *might* have originated from Euripides' *Bacchae* text. [My sequence follows Kopff's 1982 Teubner edition of the *Bacchae*. The 17 lines of my text are from *Christus Patiens* 1311, 1312, 1313, 1315, 1256, 1257, 1122, 1123, 1124, 1466, 1467, 1468, 1469, 1470, 1471, 1472, 1473.]

The 50 or so verses of Agave's speech from the *Christus Patiens* might be summarized as follows (although given the nature of the evidence even a rough outline must remain very tentative): **a)** she laments that her son has been torn to pieces; **b)** she is reluctant to embrace the body which she herself murdered; **c)** she overcomes her reluctance and kisses the parts of the corpse. [It should be noted that I place Agave's speech in the lacuna after line 1300 (following Kirk, Taplin) rather than in the lacuna after line 1329 (Dodds). As March (63, n.114) notes, "Agave's laments would fit most appropriately directly after the rising anguish of the recognition scene" (which occurs at 1282-84).]

APPENDIX TWO

The lacuna after line 1329

The gap after 1329 (about 50 lines) is hypothetically reconstructed as follows by Willink [*Classical Quarterly* 16 (1966) 46-49]: **a)** Agave's request to Cadmus to dispose of her son's corpse (1329 = the first line, then 6 missing); **b)** Cadmus' brief reply (all 3 lines missing); **c)** Dionysus' epiphany speech (40 lines missing; the last 14 are extant, being 1330-43) which Willink outlines as follows: **1.** introduction (Dionysus' vindication of himself and his mother Semele); **2.** statement of wrongs; **3.** punishment of Pentheus and the Theban people; **4.** fates of Cadmus' daughters; **5.** fate of Agave; **6.** fate of Cadmus (= lines 1330-43). Various portions of these three speeches can be reconstructed from three sources: the *Christus Patiens* (12th c. A.D.), the Antinoopolis Papyrus [= A.P.] 24 frag. 2 a and b (5th c. A.D.) and the scholiast (an Alexandrian commentator) to Aristophanes' *Wealth* line 907. The 42 lines of my translation (in the body of the text, following Willink's hypothetical reconstruction) are from: **a)** C.P. 1011, C.P. 1123, Scholiast **b)** A.P. 24, 2a, 2-4, **c)** A.P. 24, 2a, 5-7. C.P. 1639, 1640, 1360, 1361, 1362, 1664, 1663, 1667, 1668, 300, 1669, 1672, 1678, *Bacchae* 229, *Bacchae* 230, C.P. 1674, 1675, 1676, 1677, A.P. 24, 2b, 1-7, C.P. 1689.

APPENDIX THREE

Genealogy Chart for Euripides' *Bacchae*

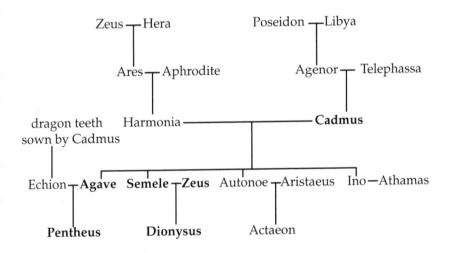

APPENDIX FOUR

THE ROMAN BID TO CONTROL BACCHIC WORSHIP
Valerie M. Warrior

Introduction

In 186 BC, some two hundred and twenty years after the production in Athens of Euripides' *Bacchae*, the Roman Senate issued a mandate, the *senatus consultum de Bacchanalibus* (decree of the Senate concerning Bacchic rites) that was intended to control the worship of Bacchus or Dionysus throughout Italy.[1] Two major sources concerning the Roman episode survive: a bronze tablet inscribed in archaic Latin that includes a letter addressed by the Roman consuls to Rome's Italian allies incorporating the Senate's decree; and a complex narrative written more than one hundred fifty years after the event by the historian Livy (59 BC-AD 17) in his *History of Rome*.[2] Livy's narrative is a moralizing set-piece so embellished with romantic elements deriving from Greek New Comedy and sensational descriptions of cult excesses that it is difficult to distinguish fact from fiction. The contemporary evidence of the inscription corroborates the historicity of the episode, while also offsetting the embellishments of Livy's account.

Despite differences in historical context and literary genre, comparison of the cult as described by Livy with that portrayed in Euripides' *Bacchae* reveals a common element: opposition by a ruling power to Dionysiac worship because the cult is perceived as a threat to the established regime. The outcomes of the opposition are, however, quite different. In the *Bacchae*, King Pentheus attempts to resist the new cult by military force and is killed by the god's worshippers. In the Roman episode, the state attempts to restrict the cult by military force, killing seven thousand of the god's worshippers (Livy 39.17.6).

The Bacchic cult had long been known in Italy, coming from Etruria (to the north of Rome) and from the Greek colonies in southern Italy.[3] That the god was familiar is evident from contemporary references in Plautus (ca. 254-184 BC), the writer of Roman comedy.[4] Nevertheless in 186, the

---

[1] The Latin word *Bacchanalia* can mean either Bacchic rites or places of Bacchic worship; see *Oxford Latin Dictionary*. Translations are adapted from those of P. G. Walsh, *Livy Book XXXIX* (1994) and G. Forsythe, *Livy Book XXXIX* (1994).
[2] See the appendix of Walsh (1994) for text and translation of the Senate's decree (*CIL* 1.2. 581 = *ILS* 18); for a photo of the decree, see Plate Nine, page 15.
[3] See E. S. Gruen, "The Bacchanalian Affair," in *Studies in Greek Culture and Roman Policy* (1990) 50-1.
[4] *Amphitruo* 702 ff., *Aulularia* 406 ff., *Casina* 979 ff., *Bacchides* 52 ff., 368 ff, *Miles Gloriosus* 858. On the prevalence of the cult in Italy, see Walsh, "Making a Drama out of a Crisis," *Greece and Rome* 43 (1996) 191.

Senate, a body of ex-magistrates one of whose functions was to advise on matters affecting the state, imposed severe restrictions on Bacchic worship throughout peninsular Italy. The penalty for infraction was death. The two consuls (chief executive officers) were ordered to conduct a special investigation. A witch-hunt ensued. Such action was unprecedented in a culture that assimilated new cults with no apparent problem.[1] For the Romans religion was politics, an integral part of the state.[2] Thus the Senate was empowered to advise on both political and religious matters, a factor that makes it difficult to define in modern terms the precise intent of the *senatus consultum de Bacchanalibus*.

The stipulations of the senatorial decree

The first stipulation on the inscription is that no one should consent to conduct a Bacchic rite. Livy is more specific: no person initiated into the Bacchic rite should consent to assemble for ceremonies, nor perform any such ritual (39.14.8). Exception, however, could be granted if certain procedures and conditions were met. Both sources specify that application must be made to the city praetor (an official in charge of judicial matters) who would refer the matter to the Senate. A decision would then be given, provided there was a quorum of one hundred senators. Meeting such requirements would have been both time-consuming and expensive, particularly for people living more than a day's journey from Rome.

The inscription prohibits any man to be in the presence of female Bacchic worshippers unless they appeared before the city praetor. No man is to be a priest, no man or woman master of ceremonies, and no one is to administer a common fund. The worshippers must consist of no more than two men and three women. Livy merely reports that the number of people who could participate was restricted to five, noting that there was to be no common fund, master of sacrifices or priest (39.18.8-9). The Senate evidently regarded participation in Bacchic worship by more than five persons as dangerous; likewise the gender composition of the gatherings, the existence of a common fund, and a hierarchy. Prescription of the death penalty indicates the gravity of the perceived threat.

That we would define this threat as political rather than religious is apparent from the inscription's legalistic language: "no one should seek to conspire, exchange vows, promises or guarantees, nor seek to exchange a pledge of loyalty" and "no one is to practise rituals in secret, or seek to celebrate them publicly, privately or outside the city." Livy's emphasis is

---

[1] As W. Burkert notes, "there is nothing comparable in religious history before the persecutions of the Christians," *Ancient Mystery Cults* (1987) 52.

[2] A. Watson: "The Roman state and religion were intertwined.... On this approach, what has to be stressed is the utility of religion to the state." *The State, Law and Religion: Pagan Rome* (1992) 58.

on conspiracy (*coniuratio*, "a swearing together for a common purpose").[1]
In the inscription, any places of Bacchic worship "other than what is sacred" are to be demolished within ten days. Livy's version is more general: the Senate ordered the destruction of Bacchanalia throughout Rome and Italy except for any ancient altar or statue consecrated there (39.18.7). The Senate intended to control the Bacchic cult without suppressing it entirely.

Livy's account of the Bacchanalian episode

Three sections are apparent: an introduction, the story of how the authorities learned of the problem, and a narrative of the actions taken in response to the revelations of the informer, Hispala Faecenia. Sensationalism is achieved by repetition of the cult excesses.

The episode opens with the dramatic announcement: "the following year diverted the consuls from the administration of armies, wars and provinces to take punitive measures against a domestic conspiracy" (39.8.1). In a phrase reminiscent of Euripides' description of Bacchus as a "wizard and enchanter from the Lydian land" (*Bacchae* 234), Livy reports that the cult had been brought from Etruria by an obscure Greek, a "petty priest and prophet" (39.8.4-5). The cult excesses are listed: pleasures of wine and feasts, intoxication, darkness, mingling of men and women, poisonings and murders within the cult (39.8.5-8) . As A. J. Toynbee notes, "The bacchants' alleged crimes were, and are, common form in the dossier for justifying the persecution of a religious sect or a political party."[2] Peculiarly Roman, however, are the allegations of indiscriminate debauchery of free-born boys and women, perjury by witnesses, falsifed seals, wills, and declarations (39.8.7).

There follows a romanticized story of how this information came to the attention of the authorities. The names are authentic but the characters and much of the plot resemble those of Greek New Comedy.[3] A young man, Publius Aebutius, was about to be initiated into the Bacchic rites in fulfilment of a vow made by his mother. His lover, the prostitute Hispala Faecenia, begged him to refuse, describing aspects of the cult which she herself knew from having earlier attended the rites as a slave with her mistress. Allegations of violence, debauchery and the drowning of cries of protest by the sound of howling, cymbals and drums (39.10.6-8) evoke the stereotypical Bacchic scenario. New, however, is the assertion that no one over the age of twenty had been initiated during the past two years.

Aebutius' refusal resulted in his being driven from home. He consulted the consul Spurius Postumius Albinus. Hispala revealed that origi-

---

[1] On the recurrence of *coniuratio* ("conspiracy") and its cognates, see Livy 39.8.1 and 3, 13.13, 14.4 and 8, 15.10, 16.3 and 5, 17.6.

[2] A. J. Toynbee, "Religious responses to spiritual ordeals," in *Hannibal's Legacy*, vol. 2 (1965) 394.

[3] A. Scafuro, "Livy's Comic Narrative of the Bacchanalia," *Helios* 16 (1989) 119-142.

nally the rituals were restricted to women and initiations held only by day. All this, however, had been changed by Paculla Annia, a priestess from Campania in central Italy, who had been the first to initiate men. The rites were held by night and the number of initiation days increased. Details of cult excesses ensue, including allegations of a larger number of homosexual than heterosexual rapes and sacrifice of those who refused to participate. Hispala's descriptions of men prophesying with frantic jerking of their bodies and of Roman matrons dressed as Bacchants, their hair flowing freely, plunging sulphurous torches into Rome's Tiber river (39.13.12) are calculated to arouse fears about non-Roman behavior. The political implications of the affair are underscored by Hispala's declaration that the number of participants was huge, "almost a second citizen body", including men and women of the nobility.

The consul reported the matter to the Senate which ordered the consuls to conduct an extraordinary investigation, offering rewards to informants and seeking out priests of the cult in Rome and throughout Italy. After taking measures to police the city and guard against arson, the consuls summoned a meeting of the people. In a dramatic speech attributed to the consul Postumius, Livy gives full rein to his rhetorical expertise. The ancestral Roman gods are contrasted with those deities who, "by means of goads implanted by the Furies, spur minds enslaved by debased and alien rites to perform every kind of crime and lustful deed" (39.15.2-3). Also mentioned are "many thousands" of worshippers of whom a high proportion were women, others being males "indistinguishable from women, rabid debauchers and debauchees" (39.15.9).

Roman rules for public assembly are contrasted with the nocturnal Bacchic meetings attended by both men and women. Reference to the age of initiation of males leads to questioning the suitability of initiates for military service and their willingness to fight on behalf of the chastity of their wives and children. Danger to the state becomes explicit as the consul declares: "Daily the evil swells and creeps in. It is already too great to be purely a private matter. Its objective involves the whole state" (39.16.3). Emphasis shifts from the political to the religious. The consul finally declares: "Men most learned in all law, divine and human, used to judge that there was nothing so inclined to the destruction of religion as sacrifices offered with foreign rather than Roman ritual." Thus articulated is the crux of the problem: the threat to traditional Roman ways, the *mos maiorum*. Punishment of the miscreants and rewards for informers conclude the episode.

Fact versus fiction

With the exception of the consul Postumius, the historicity of the characters in Livy's account cannot be confirmed. Some names, however, are authentic since magistrates bearing the family name of Aebutius, his mother and step-father are attested for the early second century BC.[1] The introduction from Etruria of night festivals and extension of initiation to men and women by the anonymous Greek mentioned at the beginning of Livy's account (39.8.3) seem authentic and are also compatible with Paculla Annia's activities in Campania.

Implausible, however, is the apparent suddenness of the Senate's action. As North has observed, "It looks very much as if what happened in 186 was not that the senate discovered something it did not know, but that it decided to act against something it knew all too well."[2] New forms of Bacchic worship that had developed in Campania and Etruria were becoming prevalent in Rome itself. The congregation of considerable numbers of males and females taking part in rituals that were held by night was perceived as a threat to the established regime, the *mos maiorum*. The Senate, therefore, exercised its prerogative to advise on matters affecting the state, passing a decree that would control but not eradicate the original cult.

The historical context

The key to the Bacchanalian episode lies in understanding the changed social and economic conditions in Italy after the Second Punic War against Carthage, a major power in North Africa. The Carthaginian general Hannibal had invaded Italy in 218 and remained there until 203. Rome's armies were engaged in this struggle not only in Italy, but also in Spain, Sicily, Greece and finally Africa where Hannibal was defeated in 202. In 200, the Romans declared war on King Philip V of Macedon and invaded Greece. The victorious Roman troops evacuated Greece in 194, only to return two years later when Greece was invaded by Antiochus III of Syria. The Romans drove him out and crossed to Asia Minor where peace was made in 188. Wars were also fought during these years in northern Italy, Liguria and Spain. The Romans had been waging war for more than thirty years.

Hannibal's prolonged presence in Italy had caused devastation and depopulation in rural areas. Many men of military age did not return to their homes, preferring to serve in the new wars. Livy reports that in 186 colonies recently planted on both the west and east coasts of Italy were deserted (39.23.3). The next year a serious slave uprising in southeastern Italy occasioned an investigation into a "conspiracy" (39.29.8-9). In 184 and 181, investigations of alleged poisonings were ordered (39.38.3 and 40.37.4-9). In the latter year, there was a further investigation of Bacchanalia (40.19.9-10). Such evidence of social disruption indicates an environment offering ample scope for the spread of a cult with a more personal appeal than that

---

[1] For a summary of the evidence, see Walsh (1996) 195-7.
[2] J. A. North, "Religious Toleration in Republican Rome," *Proceedings of the Cambridge Philological Society* 25 (1979) 88.

of the traditional gods of Roman state religion.

With the successful conclusion of the eastern wars, the Senate turned its attention to Italy, viewing the outbreak of new forms of Bacchic worship as politically dangerous. A state of emergency was declared throughout Italy which infringed upon the jurisdiction of the local magistrates.[1] The resurgence of Bacchic worship had given the Senate an opportunity to reassert the control it had exercised over Italy during the war against Hannibal.

---

[1] See A. H. McDonald, "Rome and the Italian Confederation (200-186 B.C.)," *Journal of Roman Studies* 34 (1944) 11-33, especially 13-16.

GLOSSARY OF IMPORTANT THEMES AND TERMS

Actaeon: paradigm of the hunter who becomes the hunted on account of his *hybris*. Actaeon boasted that he was a better hunter than Artemis, goddess of hunting. For this offense Artemis transformed the young man into a stag. He was then torn apart by his own hounds who did not recognize their master. Actaeon was Pentheus' first cousin. But Pentheus did not learn from his cousin's tragic fate (cp. 337-40).

Bacchae: (Greek *Bakchai*, Latin *Bacchae*, whence the play's title): bacchantes or women possessed by Bacchus. Cp. 'Maenads' below.

Bacchus: another name for Dionysus and the one by which the Romans knew him. The god's worshipper could also be called 'Bacchus' (*Bacchae* 491), a phenomneon paralleled nowhere else in Greek religion [Burkert 1985, 162]. The word, certainly non-Greek, may well be Lydian in origin.

Bromios: ('the Roarer') one of Dionysus' more common names in poetry (cp. 65n.). Roaring was characteristic of the god and his cult. He was born from Zeus' roaring thunder. Dionysus himself roars (151), being the god of the bull (100, 618, 920, 1159). The tambourine-like drums of his maenads also roar (155) as does their flute (161).

Cadmus: a) the myth of the 'Sown Men': After a long and futile search for his sister Europa, Cadmus the Phoenician ended up in Thebes (cp. 264n.). The city was guarded by a dragon sacred to Ares. At Athena's advice Cadmus slew the dragon and sowed half its teeth in the earth. From these sown teeth there sprang forth miraculously from the earth a band of armed warriors. They fought among themselves until only five survived, of whom Pentheus' father Echion ('Snake-Man') is the most famous (cp. 538-44). With these five earthborn Sown Men Cadmus founded Thebes.

b) Cadmus as therapist; his 'treatment' of the mad Agave (1263-1300): "Seeking to divert Agave from fantasy to reality, Cadmus first attracts her attention to an aspect of external reality which is not only *not* charged with anxiety and with subjective preoccupations but is, in Greek belief, a beneficial phenomenon which dispels fantasies and neutralises nightmares: the sunny, luminous sky... She begins to react to the apotropaic value of the Sun, whose brilliance probably reminds her that the time of (violent) nocturnal rites is past." [Devereux 41]

Chorus: composed of fifteen Asiatic Bacchae, played by men wearing wigs; women could not be actors. The youthful, physically vigorous Bacchae sang and danced to the music of a reed-piper. Their odes are composed of sets of linguistically complex stanzas that 'respond' to one another metrically and choreographically, the first stanza being called a *strophe* ('turn'), the second an *anti-strophe* ('counter-turn').

Dionysiac virtues: The two main ones for the chorus are tranquility and prudent thinking (390); the latter leads to the former. These virtues, which keep disaster away, contrast with Pentheus' rashness and frantic exertions (esp. 616-37). [Leinieks 278-80]

Dionysus: a) various domains of his power in the *Bacchae*: god of the bull (100, 618, 920, 1017, 1159), earthquakes (585), everyman (206-9, 420-23), frenzy (33, 851), grape-vine (12), ivy (81), liberation (443-48, 497-98, 609-22, 642-49), lightning (1083; cp. 595), liquid nature (704-11), self-transformation (477-78), theater (658, 925-44n.), trees (1074, 1110-12), wine (278-85, 422-23).

   b) Dionyus as democratic god *par excellence*: (cp. 421n.) "He is accessible to all, not like Pythian Apollo through priestly intermediaries, but directly in his gift of wine and through membership of his cult group. His worship probably made its original appeal mainly to people who had no citizen rights in the aristocratic 'gentile state' and were excluded from the older cults associated with the great families. And in the classical age it seems to have retained a good deal of this popular character." [Dodds 127]

   c) Dionysus' name and its meaning: In the first two lines of the play the sequence *Dios...Dionysos* etymologizes the name Dio-nysus from *Dios*, the possessive case of Zeus' name. This word-play (also at 27, 466, 550-51, 859-60) emphasizes immediately the important fact of Dionysus' descent from Zeus. The origin of the second half of the name Dio-*nysus* is unknown, though very probably non-Greek. Folk etymology had Dionysus' name mean 'Zeus of Mt. Nysa.'

   d) Dionysus' androgyny: 1] *in literature*: It is not Euripides' invention. Aeschylus' *Edonians* has Dionysus taunted by Lycurgus as "a womanish man" (*gynnis*); and his *Theoroi* has Dionysus complain about how the satyrs scoff at him: "that I am not skilled in working with iron, but am a cowardly, womanish man (*gynnis*), and am not to be counted among the males." These fragments suggest that

Aeschylus had Dionysus dressed in disguise. Pentheus in the *Bacchae* (353) calls him "the effeminate looking stranger." [Cp. Dodds 133; Seaford 1996, 180] **2]** *in art*: During the archaic and early classical periods Dionysus appears in vase painting and sculpture as an older, dignified god, with a beard, a long robe, a crown of ivy and his special wine cup. By 450 B.C. the god becomes more youthful and effeminate and he is usually naked and beardless. **3]** *explanation:* Dionysus' androgyny derives at least in part from the ritual transvestism of his male worshippers [Seaford 1996, 180; cp. Dodds 133-34]

e) Dionysus' physical appearance: an effeminate costume (353), long curly golden hair (235, 455, 493), white skin (457), wine-colored cheeks (236, 438). In his disguise as the Stranger from Lydia he later (433 ff.) makes himself out to be a servant of Dionysus and the cult leader of an Asiatic chorus of female devotees. Accordingly from the outset he wears full bacchic regalia (fawnskin cloak and ivy wreath) and carries a thyrsus (240, 495-96). He maintains this disguise until near the end.

f) Dionysus' divinity, proofs: Dionysus presents to Pentheus several significant manifestations of his godhood: **1]** the 'conversion' of Cadmus and Tiresias (170-369); **2]** the miraculous escape of the maenads from jail in Thebes (443-48); **3]** the Stranger's initiation by Dionysus himself in the Bacchic mysteries (461-518); **4]** the 'palace miracles,' especially the earthquake (585-637); **5]** the series of 'miracles' attending the maenads on Cithaeron (677-774). None of these gradually more explicit 'warnings' persuade Pentheus (cp. 649). At 789-809 the Stranger gives his opponent one last chance by offering to bring the maenads peacefully from Cithaeron to Thebes.

g) Dionysus' smiling mask: Dionysus apparently wore a smiling mask (so 380, 439, and 1020 suggest). Such masks are very unusual in tragedy, though perhaps it was a convention for gods, or at least for Dionysus. The god's smile was, however, "an ambiguous smile — here (439) the smile of a martyr, afterwards the smile of the destroyer (1020)." [Dodds 131]. Dionysus' smile and laughter were traditional in vase-painting and literature. [Cp. Kirk 61; Foley 126-33]

h) Dionysus' bizarre predictions at lines 1330-39: 1] the transformation of Cadmus and Harmonia into snakes (1330-31). **2]** the exile of Cadmus and Harmonia to a foreign land (1333-34; cp. 1354-55). **3]** the ascendance of Cadmus to leader of a foreign army (1334; cp. 1356), presumably the Encheleis or 'Eels' from Illyria (on the Yugoslavian coast). **4]** the attack of Cadmus and his army against Greece (1335; cp. 1356-60) and their subsequent disaster upon sacking Delphi (1335-37). **5]** the deliverance of Cadmus and Harmonia by Ares to the islands of the Blessed (1338-9). [Dodds 235-36] These strange predictions are "an extreme example of a common device in Euripides, who connected the outcome of many of his plays with known cults, rituals and practices." [Kirk 134] But Leinieks [338] argues interestingly that the predictions at 1333-38 and 1354-62 are later interpolations inspired by an historical event, namely the Gallic invasion of Greece and their subsequent defeat at Delphi in 279 B.C.

i) Dionysus as a pagan rival of Christ: *Similarities:* Both gods presented the world with a mystery religion that was full of miracles; both conquered death, both obscured the distinction between blood and wine, both promised their followers salvation after death. [Henrichs 1984, 212-13]. *Differences:* "the son of God took on human form to save mankind, with terrible consequences for himself...Dionysos takes on human form as one of several disguises, often with more than a hint of humour, and the form has nothing to do with his divinity. In other words, there is nothing inherently important about his human form and nothing inherently admirable about his human behaviour." [Carpenter 120; cp. Evans 145-73] For an image of Christ as Dionysus see plate 10 on p. 17 of the Introduction.

Dithyramb: Dionysus' special song (cp. 526n.), performed by choruses at revelries of wine, music, and wild abandonment. This (non-Greek) noun first occurs in the lyric poet Archilochus (c. 650 B.C): "Since I know how to begin the beautiful song of lord Dionysus, the dithyramb, once I have been thunder-struck in my mind by wine" (frag.120 W). Aristotle argued plausibly that tragedy originated in the dithyramb (*Poetics* ch. 4).

Drum: (*tympanon*) the play's main musical instrument, carried by the chorus of Asian maenads (cp. 58n.), was a small wooden hoop (12-20 inches in diameter) resembling a tambourine but covered on *both* sides with hide. It was struck by the knuckles of the right hand as it was held upright in the left. Percussion instruments were considered exotic by the Greeks and used mainly in the cults of Dionysus and Cybele. The *tympanon* was imported from the East and played primarily by women.

Earthquake: During the first of the 'palace miracles' an earthquake shakes Pentheus' palace (583-93, 623). This miracle was probably not Euripides' invention. Aeschylus wrote a trilogy about a Thracian king Lycurgus, who, like Pentheus, took Dionysus captive and was subsequently driven mad and torn to pieces. One fragment (58 R) suggests an earthquake-like scenario: "The palace (of Lycurgus) is possessed by the god, the roof revels like the Bacchae." Given the simplicity of fifth century stage mechanisms, effects such as those described at *Bacchae* 592-93 (columns reeling) were probably meant to be conjured in the mind's eye (cp. the storms in *King Lear* and *The Tempest*). Although one building (the stables of 618) is said to collapse (633), this is to be imagined as at the back of the royal complex (i.e. off-stage). The palace facade remains standing (639, 646) which probably explains why Pentheus never comments on any damage to his residence.

God-fighter: (*theo-machos*) The *Bacchae* contains the first surviving occurrences of this important word (45, 325, 1255) which appears nowhere else in tragedy, thus suggesting that it was coined by Euripides. The prototype of the god-fighter is Lycurgus, a king of Thrace who tried, like Pentheus, to drive the new religion of Dionysus out of his country. His attempt ended in death (*Iliad* 6. 128-43). Aeschylus told the same story in a lost trilogy, *Lycurgeia*. Other such rebels include Tantalus and Sisyphus (*Odyssey* 11. 582-600), Prometheus and Pentheus (Aeschylus), Ajax (Sophocles), Hippolytus and Bellerophon (Euripides).

Happiness: (*eudaimonia*) an important word, occurring more often (9x) than in any other Greek tragedy. *Eu-daimonia* means being in the proper relationship to divinity. At the root of *eudaimonia* is the noun *daimôn* which is an anonymous supernatural power who apportions one's individual destiny. True happiness often seems impossible in Greek drama. Thus the messenger in Euripides' *Medea* (1228-30): "Of mortals there is no one who is happy (*eudaimôn*). Wealth might pour in and make one man luckier than another, but he cannot be happy (*eudaimôn*)." *Daimôn* can can also refer to one's 'destiny' as in the famous fragment (119) of the Presocratic philosopher Heraclitus (c. 500 B.C.): "Man's character (*êthos*) determines his destiny (*daimôn*)." Democritus, another Presocratic philosopher (c. 470 B.C.), suggests, as did Plato later, that "Happiness (*eudaimonia*) does not reside in cattle nor in gold. The soul is the house of a man's destiny (*daimôn*)." (frag. 171).

Helping friends, harming enemies: the primary tenet of moral thought from Homer to Plato (cp. 879-80n.). The lyric poet Archilochus (c. 650 B.C.) wrote: "I know how to love my friend and hate and revile my enemy." (frag. 23.14-15W). This long-standing tradition of equating justice with retaliation (*Iliad* 9.613-15; *Ody.* 6.184-85) was first challenged overtly by Socrates in Plato's *Republic* (I, 335 D). Four hundred years later Jesus challenged it: "You have heard it said, 'You shall love your neighbor and hate your enemy.' But I say to you, 'Love your enemies and pray for those who persecute you. If you welcome only your brothers, what extraordinary deed are you doing? Don't even the pagans do as much?' " (Matthew 5. 43-45) And similarly, "To the man who strikes your cheek, offer him the other as well."(Luke 6.29) Jesus' golden rule was antici-pated by Yahweh's words to Moses: "You must love your neigh-bor as yourself." (*Leviticus* 19.18)

Hybris: wanton disregard of decency, violence in word or deed, or inso-lent transgression. Acts of *hybris* involve the deliberate or self-in-dulgent abuse of power (esp. by the strong and proud) at the ex-pense of another's honor. Two examples: the usurpation of Odysseus' estate in Ithaca by Penelope's suitors and Ajax's boast-ing that he did not need Athena's help in battle, on account of which she drove him mad (Sophocles' *Ajax* 770-78). The concept of *hybris*, which is closely related to satiety, extends beyond humans and gods. Plants can be hybristic by growing over-abundantly (*Bacchae* 113), animals by being unruly (*Bacchae* 743) and rivers by over-flowing. The opposite of *hybris* is *sôphrosynê* (moderation, self-con-trol, wisdom), the characteristic virtue of Dionysiac cult.

Hybris occurs more often in the *Bacchae* than in any other trag-edy (14x, matched only by *Ajax*). Usually it registers the anger of Dionysus and his chorus at the insults of Pentheus (374, 516, 555; contrast 247, 779) and others. Dionysus' revenge against the Thebans is the result of their *hybris* in not believing his divinity (1297, 1347).

Iacchus: a mystic name of Dionysus at Athens and Eleusis (home of the mysteries of Demeter and Persephone). The name Iacchus (725) is probably related to *iachein*, 'to give a ritual cry.' At line 149 Bacchus spurs straggling worshippers with his *iache*, 'shout of joy'.

Initiation: 1) initiation = status dramatization or (irreversible) change of status via ritual; 2) initiate = one who has already undergone initiation; 3) initiand = the candidate for initiation. [Burkert 1987, 8 and 136 n. 33] Why is Dionysus "most terrifying" in the ritual of initiation (860-61)? Because the initiands must undergo the terrors of the ritual death that preceded the spiritual rebirth at the heart of the Dionysiac mysteries. [Seaford 1981, 261]

Irony: an incongruity or discrepancy between a) words and their mean-ing; b) actions and their results (or situations and their outcomes). The element of contrast is essential to both modes and usually in-volves a contrast between appearance and reality. One of irony's main functions is to be a witting or unwitting instrument of truth, a reminder of the reality behind the semblance or delusion. As sug-gested above, there are two main types of irony:

a) verbal irony: the use of words to convey the opposite of their lit-eral meaning, i.e. saying what one does not mean. Within this category there are two main types: **1]** *unconscious irony*: the speaker fails to understand the inner meaning of his/her own words. Sophocles made this type of irony famous in *Oedipus the King*. Examples in the *Bacchae* cluster around Pentheus' boasting (e.g. 491). **2]** *conscious irony*: the speaker intentionally uses his/her superior knowledge to toy with the victim or propel the victim to doom by a *double entendre*. The notorious ambiguity of Apollo's Delphic oracles exemplify well this type of irony. Examples in the *Bacchae* cluster around the revenge of the master plotter Dionysus against Pentheus (e.g. 494, 496, 498, 500, 502, 518, 961-72). **3]** In both unconscious and conscious irony the double meaning (explicit vs. implicit) is usually known to the audience. Indeed much of their pleasure derives from their omniscient perspective on the failed attempts of dramatic players to escape an impending catastrophe.

b) **situational irony:** the contrast between an real and a supposed situation, between the expectation of an action or event and its fulfilment. This often consists in a clash between conflicting intrigues. Examples in the *Bacchae* cluster around Pentheus the hunter becoming the hunted or Pentheus the spectator becoming the spectacle.

Ivy: Of the six plants/trees mentioned in the *Bacchae* [ivy, vine, evergreen creeper; pine, oak, fir], ivy is the most important (13x). "Because of its evergreen vitality it typifies the victory of vegetation over its enemy the winter...That it was thought of as a vehicle of the god himself seems to be implied by the worship of Dionysus as 'Ivy-lord'...." [Dodds 77] In sum, ivy symbolized the god's presence and power. Without a crown of ivy a thyrsus was not a real thyrsus, nor was a maenad without a crown of ivy a real maenad (cp. 81n). The twisting pattern of ivy was thought by the ancients to imitate the Dionysiac dance.

Last lines of the play (1388-92): Are they genuine? Whereas modern theater has the 'final curtain' as its boundary line between the play and the outside world, Greek theater must use words to identify closure. All eighteen surviving plays of Euripides end with a tailpiece by the chorus; five have virtually the same ending. Controversy surrounds the genuineness of these endings. The main arguments against authenticity are as follows: a) the repetition of endings indicates tampering; b) in four of the five plays the lines seem inappropriate and banal. The arguments for authenticity are: a) the repetition of endings marks them not as defective but rather as a signature of Euripides' tragic consciousness; b) the lines are indeed appropriate to any play like the *Bacchae* which contains a marked reversal of fortune. Both these sets of arguments are inadequate because both are grounded in a) highly subjective notions of appropriateness or banality; b) the unexamined assumption that the final choral tag must have some deep moral or thematic significance. It is more probable that Euripides' formulaic tail-pieces are meant to serve primarily as conventional and self-identifying markers of closure. [cp. Dunn 1996, 17]

Laughter as a lethal weapon: The competitiveness of Greek society dictated that one person's victory came at another's expense. Losing the contest meant 'losing face' before one's peers; this had to be avoided at all costs. Euripides' Medea, rejected by Jason for a younger woman, murders her beloved sons because "it is unbearable to be laughed at by one's enemies" (797). Even the gods share this attitude: Athena says to Odysseus "Well, isn't laughing in the face of your enemies the sweetest laughter?" (*Ajax* 79). These sentiments reveal well the Greek moral code of 'helping friends, harming enemies.' Within this general cultural context "Pentheus is unique in that, while the typical tragic character fears scorn, *he* dispenses it; not only at Teiresias and Cadmus (250, 322)...but also at the story of Dionysus' birth (286), at his divine rites and celebrants (1081), and even at the god himself (272, 1081). His readiness to use laughter offensively (5 instances is an unparalleled frequency), to assume a superior stance, sets him up for a fall, which comes appropriately at the hands of a god who himself is described as 'smiling' during his arrest (439) and is urged on to the human hunt, ironically, with a 'smiling visage' (1021)...There are in all 10 *gelôs* ('laughter') words in the *Bacchae*, the most in any Euripidean play..." [Dillon 1991, 347-51].

Maenads: Frenzied female devotees of Dionysus (usually married women). More specifically, maenads were "female followers of Dionysus who were differentiated from ordinary worshippers by their ceremonial garb, their ritual activites and, if their name is any indication, their exalted state of mind. In short, they were the practioners of ritual maenadism, the most fascinating branch of Dionsyiac cult." [Henrichs 1982, 143] As lines 135-39 indicate the three main activities of maenadic ritual were: *oreibasia*, the maenads going to the mountain to dance, an event which took place every other winter; *sparagmos*, tearing-to-pieces an animal; *omophagia*, devouring of the animal's raw flesh by Dionysus (not by the maenads, as is commonly thought); hence his epithet 'Raw-Eater.'

The word 'maenad' is derived from *mania*, 'madness' or 'frenzy'; hence *mainades* are 'mad women.' The Greek noun *mania* denotes "frenzy, not as the ravings of delusion, but as its etymological connection with *menos* [might, force; spirit, passion] would suggest, as an experience of intensified mental power." [Burkert 1985, 162] How 'mad' were the maenads? "No immediate answer to this urgent question is available... By all indications, the peculiar religious identity of the maenads had more to do with sweat and physical exhaustion than with an abnormal state of mind. To exhaust oneself for Dionysus became a 'sweet toil' (*Bacchae* 66f.), a source of exhilaration and relief. Once that elation had been achieved by ritual means, the maenads came down from their mountain, resumed their normal lives, and waited for the return of the ritual two years later." [Henrichs 1982, 144-47] Euripides' play describes *mythic* maenads, not historical ones. 'Maenads' is used thirteen times of the *Theban* Bacchae and only once of the *Asian* Bacchae (601n.). As the play progresses and the Theban maenads become more frenzied the frequency of the word increases dramatically. As the example of Agave illustrates, their frenzy is forced upon them and is temporary rather than permanent. The word 'maenad' was "essentially a poetic word which has decidedly reprehensive connotations even in the *Bacchae*... As opposed to the maenads of literature and myth, the maenads of actual cult are usually called Bakchai." [Henrichs 1982, 146-47]

Mountains: the play's six named mountains are: **Cithaeron** (4,625 feet): The *Bacchae's* most important mountain (12x) is ten miles south of Thebes and thickly wooded with firs and oaks. Being sacred to Dionysus, it represents the world of Dionysiac worship where the maenads roam freely; it is the antithesis of Pentheus' city. **Nysa:** Numerous mountains bear this name, all fictional and all associated with Dionysus. It is a mystical mountain that travelled wherever the god's cult did. The name is perhaps to be linked with the second half of the name Dio-*nysus*. **Olympus** (9,600 feet): Home of the Olympian gods, on the east coast of Thessaly separating Greece from Macedonia. From it the Olympian gods take their name since that was their camp when they fought the Titans. **Parnassus** (8,200 feet): Near the Gulf of Corinth at Cape Opus, Parnassus towers over Delphi, the spectacular site of Apollo's oracle, situated on the mountain's lower southern slopes. **Pieria:** Birthplace of the Muses in Macedonia on the northern massif of Mt. Olympus. **Tmolus** (over 6,000 feet): Sacred to Dionysus, this mountain range formed the backbone of Lydia; its lower slopes were famous for their vineyards.

Mysteries, Dionysiac: At the heart of Dionysus' mysteries was "a rite of passage centered around an extraordinary (sometimes) death-like experience that effected a transition from outside to inside the group (the *thiasos*) and from anxious ignorance to joyful knowledge, a transition in which the initial attitude of the initiand is likely to be ambivalent." [Seaford 1996, 39]. Our knowledge of the language used in mystic initiation is minimal. There is, however, inscriptional evidence from two fourth century B.C. grave mounds in south Italy (the gold 'leaves' from Thurii) which suggests that the initiand's rite of passage was veiled in riddling language. [Burkert 1985, 295] The most important evidence from the fifth century for Dionysiac mysteries is *Bacchae* 72-77 where the prerequisites for happiness are outlined: knowledge of the mysteries; living a life of purity; initiation into the cult group; and participation in the mountain rituals honoring Dionysus. This happiness depends on a religious experience *in the here and now* (72-82; 910-11). There exists strong evidence, however, that the mysteries of Dionysus promised blessedness *in the afterlife* as well [Burkert 1985, 293-95; Seaford 1996, 41]. If so, then they would resemble the Eleusinian mysteries, which honored Demeter and Persephone and promised happiness to the 'initiated' in the present life *and in the afterlife*, as we learn from the *Homeric Hymn to Demeter* (c. 675-625 B.C.): "Blessed is the mortal on earth who has seen these mysteries but whoever is uninitiated in the holy rites and has no part in them never has a share of the same joys when he is dead down in the dreary darkness." (480-82)

Pentheus: a) age: Probably 18-20 years old. He is described as a 'young man' (274, 974; cp. 1254) and appears to be just beginning to grow his first beard (1185-87). This agrees with the fact that "in vase painting he is generally beardless." [Seaford 1996, 227; contrast Leinieks 199-210].

b) Pentheus' name and its meaning: His name derives from *penthos*, 'pain', hence *Pentheus* means 'he who suffers.' Tiresias plays on this etymology three times (286-97, 298-99, 367). The Romans called such word-play *nomen omen* because the *name* carries an *omen* of one's fate. A telling example is the most famous pun in the Greek New Testament: "You are Peter (*Petros*) and upon this rock (*petra*) I shall build my church." (Matthew 16.18)

c) Pentheus' failed initiation into the Dionysiac mysteries (616-37): The young king's ordeals at 616-37 as he attempts to tie up the bull (i.e. Dionysus) resemble those of the initiand in the Eleusinian mysteries as described by the biographer Plutarch who had himself been initiated into the Dionysiac mysteries. At the moment of death, Plutarch informs us that "the soul suffers an experience like those who celebrate the great initiations...in the beginning wanderings and wearisome running around in circles and some unfinished journeys half-seen through darkness; then [just] before the consummation [come] all the terrors—panic and trembling and sweat and amazement. And after this a certain miraculous light comes upon you..." Analogous to the key features of this passage (wandering, terror, bright light) are Pentheus' initiation-like sufferings in the Dionysiac mysteries, sufferings which illuminate the *subjective* aspect of initiation, namely the initiand's ignorance, fear, and confusion: a] panting, sweating, shuddering (620-21); b] wild rushing about (625-28); c] darkness (628; cp. 510, 611); d] a sudden epiphany of miraculous light (630-31), symbolizing the presence of the god; e] exhaustion (635). Just as the guilt-haunted wanderings of Orestes in Aeschylus' *Oresteia* and those of Oedipus in Sophocles' *Oedipus at Colonus* have aptly been likened to the wanderings of the not-yet-initiated, so too could Pentheus' 'wanderings' here be likened. Unlike Pentheus, whose rite of passage into the joy and knowledge of the mysteries fails, the chorus succeeds, passing through the fearful experiences of initiation (604-9) until they see 'the light' (608) of the liberated Dionysus; cp. 609n. [Seaford 1981, 255-57; 1996, 201].

d) **Pentheus' passion (*erôs*) to see the maenads on Cithaeron:** At line 813 the Stranger (Dionysus) asks Pentheus why he has fallen into so great a 'passion' (*erôs*) to see the Theban Bacchae on the mountain. Why does the Stranger use such a striking word here, the strongest Greek word for sexual desire (though *erôs* is often not sexual) and one which appears only here in the play? Here is a psychoanalytic perspective on Pentheus' *erôs*: "The immediate occasion of Dionysus' assertion of power over Pentheus is the latter's acknowledgment of his erotic impulses toward the women in his mother's entourage, women who...are surrogates for the desired mother. Indeed some of the energy in Pentheus' animus against the maenads comes from the ambivalence created by his repressed infantile desire to possess his mother (and, in this case, her collective substitute). Aspiring to adult masculinity, Pentheus wants to possess and master these women who directly threaten that male superiority; and the assertion of sexual, political, and military authority comes to the same thing." [Segal 1986, 283] Here is a ritual perspective: "This sudden ambivalent passion (*erôs*) may seem odd, but it is one of several respects in which the experiences of Pentheus reflect mystic initiation" (since the strong desire for mystic initiation might be called *erôs*, as it is in Aeschylus frag. 387: "I shuddered with passionate desire (*erôs*) for this mystic rite of completion.") [Seaford 1996, 213]

e) **Pentheus as 'Peeping Tom'?** To describe him as such [Dodds xliii] is to suggest that his behavior is that of a sexually perverted voyeur. That is not the case. The herdsmen, from their hiding places in the bushes, also spied on the Bacchae. Certainly Pentheus is sexually curious. He has a 'passionate desire' (813) to see the maenads and is described as 'spectator', 'spy', and 'searcher' of the women on the mountain. And he does harp on the idea of the Bacchae going off to the mountain to drink wine and serve the lusts of men. But to characterize him in neo-Freudian language as "the dark puritan whose passion is compounded of horror and unconscious desire and it is this which leads him to his ruin" [Dodds 97] goes too far [Oranje 40-43, 54, 82; Seaford 1996, 33]. He is rather a lonely young man (962-63) with virtually no sexual knowledge [March 58].

f) **Pentheus as transvestite:** Why does Pentheus disguise himself as a woman? At 823-24 the primary reason given is physical safety; he must look like a maenad lest he be killed. "This clearly implies that in the rite described by Euripides only women take part in the Dionysiac dance. A male is allowed to participate in the dance only if he is ritually turned into a woman by means of ritual transvestism." [Leinieks 51] At 854-55 the *dramatic* reason given for Pentheus' cross-dressing is to humiliate the king before his people in the streets of his city. But since this explanation contradicts 841 (where the Stranger says he will lead Pentheus on deserted streets) and since Pentheus was willing to go without disguise in the first place (818), it appears that the plot did not require the king to cross-dress. Rather it seems that the disguise was a traditional feature of the story whose original motive was probably *ritual* [Dodds 181; cp. Kirk 93-94]. In other words, Pentheus cross-dresses because transvestism is a well-known feature of initiation rites and its function in those rites is "to deprive the initiand of his previous identity so that he may assume a new one." [Seaford 1981, 259; 1996, 222] In this case, of course, Pentheus as the initiand "takes on the very attributes of his alter ego that he most scorns...and acts out the opposite of the values of his male peer group: effeminacy instead of masculinity; emotionality instead of rationality; illusion, magic, and trickery instead of realistic clarity, forthrightness, and martial discipline." [Segal 1997, 171]

g) **Pentheus' double vision (918-19):** Why does Pentheus see two suns and two seven-gated cities of Thebes? At least two reasons, one physical, one religious. Dionysus has sent "a light-headed frenzy" (851) upon him which may well have caused distorted vision. Furthermore, Pentheus, as a new initiand into the Dionysiac cult group (*thiasos*), is assuming a new identity [Seaford 1981, 259-60]. His double vision as well as his seeing the bull (920-22) fit in with his earlier vision of Dionysus as a bull (618-19) and as a 'light' (630) during his initiatory experiences in the palace. Seaford [1996, 223-

24] even suggests that Pentheus, in this new role as a Dionysiac initiand, "sees what he ought to see" (924) because he is holding a sacred and perhaps secret object, namely a mystic mirror. Such obscurely reflecting mirrors were apparently used in Orphic and Dionysiac mysteries to stimulate and confuse the initiate. By looking into such a mirror Pentheus would see two suns, two Thebes and the Stranger at his side *as well as* Dionysus in the shape of a bull. Foley [129-30] observes that "the audience also sees double in this scene although in a different way. On stage are two figures wearing long robes, two wigs of long curls, two figures carrying the same Dionysiac paraphernalia. The sacrificial victim of the god... has visually become almost the ritual double he often seems to have been in religious and literary tradition."

h) Pentheus' vision of Dionysus as a bull (920-22): Pentheus sees the god in his animal manifestation. But does he see the Stranger *as well as* the bull-god? Yes say some [Dodds 193; Seaford 1996, 224]; no say others [Kirk 101, Oranje 89, 142]. Whichever is the case, "the vision is no drunken fancy, but a sinister epiphany of the god in his bestial incarnation, comparable with the visions of medieval satanists who saw their Master with the horns of a goat." [Dodds 193]

i) Pentheus' ritual transformation (780-922): 1] He moves from excited aggression to meek subordination to his former enemy (780-809; 949-54); 2] he becomes effeminate (821-36; cp. 925-38); 3] he acquires mystic insight (918-24).

j) Pentheus as tragic comedian (925-44): The sight of the maenads' arch-enemy, himself dressed as a maenad, so intently adjusting his feminine costume (937-38), has a genuine comic element. As in the Tiresias-Cadmus scene Euripides has finely interwoven the comic and tragic. For this scene as 'meta-theater,' see 925-44n.

k) Pentheus' moment of truth? (1121): For the first time he confesses to 'errors' (*hamartia*, a concept central to Aristotle's theory of tragedy, *Poetics* 1453a8) but what he means, beyond the fact that he is in physical danger, is unclear. Perhaps he finally recognizes Dionysus' divinity, as Dionysus had predicted (860). If so, it is not through any great insight but because the god's force has overwhelmed him [cp. Leinieks 241]. Nor is it at all clear [despite Dodds 216] that Pentheus dies completely sane and sincerely repentant. As Kirk [117] puts it, "Does he see the truth of the situation? We do not know, but it seems improbable."

l) Pentheus' death and its ritual pattern: Greek initiation (puberty) rituals proceeded in three phases: 1] the boy was taken away from his community in a 'send-off procession' (*pompê*); 2] then submitted to an 'contest' or 'ordeal' (*agôn*); 3] then returned to the community in a 'triumphal procession' (*kômos*). Analogous to this sequence (departure of child from home, struggle, and return as adult) Euripides presents a Pentheus who is to be led out of Thebes by Dionysus as 'escort' (*pompos*, 965; cp. 920) to the sacred space where he will undergo an ordeal (*agôn*, 964, 975; cp. 1163) from which he will return triumphally. In fact, however, the 'ordeal' will turn out to be a deadly sacrifice and the triumphal return (*kômos*, 1167, 1172) will be made by the presiding 'priestess' (1114). Her victory prize will, at least initially, be spiritual bliss (1171, 1180, 1242; 1258). [Seaford 1981, 267-68].

m) **Pentheus' death as an animal sacrifice:** Lines 1238-40 bring to a climax a long series of details which suggest that Euripides saw Pentheus' death as following the generic pattern of a Greek animal sacrifice. I summarize the striking parallels detected by Seidensticker [1979, 90]: **1]** victim adorned for festival and made into sacred property (dressing of Pentheus; 934); **2]** victim willingly led to sacred place (Cithaeron) by escort (Dionysus; 965, 1047); **3]** at the sacred place all is made ready (1051-57); **4]** victim brought to altar (fir tree) where there is prayer (1078-81), silence (1084-7), a throwing of objects (stones, branches, thyrsi) at victim (1093-1100); **5]** after preparations are complete, sacrifice begins (1114-15); **6]** victim's death-rattle drowned by yelling of sacrificers (1131-33); **7]** victim dismembered (1125-36,1209-10,1219-21); parts prepared for feast (1184, 1242); **8]** victim's skull is set up to commemorate sacrifice (1238-40); **9]** feelings of guilt lead to punishment of sacrificer for murdering victim ('priestess' Agave expelled from Thebes). Seaford [1996, 231] suggests that "the sacrifical killing of Pentheus belongs to the play's pattern of mystic initiation, as the Dionysiac initiand might be treated like a sacrifical victim."

n) **Pentheus as scapegoat:** The dying Pentheus has been seen by some scholars as a kind of scapegoat (*pharmakos*) whose death serves as a purification of Thebes' collective guilt (cp. 963n.); similarly Sophocles' hero in *Oedipus the King* (c. 430 B.C.). As Stanford [177-78] observes, "Dressing up the victim was a regular part of the *pharmakos* ritual. Hence the dressing scene would have a grim symbolism for the spectators in Euripides' time. Nor was the symbolism dimmed in Christian days. It impressed a Byzantine writer vividly enough to move him to the elaborate Christian adaptation of the play, the *Christus Patiens* ('Suffering Christ'). The parallelism between the death of Pentheus and the death of Our Saviour is in some respects startlingly close — the Mocking in the Purple Robe, the Hanging on the Tree, the Mater Dolorosa ('Sorrowing Mother'). If we regard Pentheus as not just an obstinate tyrant, but as a scapegoat for the Old Law which knew not Bacchus, the Old Law which

120

must die to make way for the New Law, then the analogy becomes even more striking." [See further 1096-1100n.] Against this notion of Pentheus as a scapegoat see Leinieks 167-75; on Dionysus and Christ, see Evans 145-73.

Sacrifice: a) definition: the orderly (ritual) killing of animals. "Sacrifice controls, encloses within traditional form, an act of potentially disturbing violence. In this respect it is antithetical to the unpredictable violence of the hunt. Animals hunt, and may assist human hunting, but only humans sacrifice. And yet sacrificial ritual resembles in certain respects the hunt, for example in the encirclement and pelting of the victim, which in the sacrifice has become merely symbolic (ordered) violence." [Seaford 1996, 212 and 231-32] For the killing of Pentheus as an animal sacrifice, see Glossary, 'Pentheus' death.'

b) Agave's Dionysian sacrifice (1114): This is the first climax of the messenger's speech (cp. 1141). In her role as 'priestess' in this ritual tearing-to-pieces (*sparagmos*) of Pentheus Agave completely perverts the normal function of sacrifice as a means of mediation between man and god (cp. 794n, 1184, 1246-47). The pattern recalls Aeschylus' *Oresteia* where Agamemnon sacrificed his daughter Iphigeneia which led his wife Clytemnestra to sacrifice him in revenge. The situation here is more pathetic since the mad Agave does not know she is sacrificing her son. (Sacrificial killing was usually performed by males; Seaford 1996, 238).

Shame Culture vs. Guilt Culture: a) guilt vs. shame: "Guilt is that anxiety occurring when a person perceives that, either in action or thought, he is diverging from some group norm that he himself defines as intrinsically desirable... Shame, by contrast, is that form of anxiety occurring when a person perceives himself as having failed in some effort at achievement in a manner visible to others whose approval he desires." [Gouldner 83-84].

b) guilt culture vs. shame culture: This distinction is one useful way of contrasting, in large conceptual terms, the psychological complexities of modern (post-Freudian) society from the ancient Greek world, which was a heavily shame-based culture. The basic difference between these two types of cultures is "the agent or the locus of reproach. In shame cultures the reproachful party is some person other than the reproached; in guilt cultures reproach comes essentially from the *self*, so that the reproacher and the reproached are one and the same person." [Gouldner *ibid.*]

c) honor and shame: If honor is "the value of a person in his own eyes, but also in the eyes of his society," then in a culture like that of the Greeks based primarily on shame, 'what people said' represented the measuring stick of a person's worth. Ridicule by the court of public opinion diminished status and reputation, resulting in 'loss of face.' [Pitt Rivers 19]

Sophist: Originally the word referred to a man of wisdom (*sophia*), an expert in a particular craft (e.g. music, divination). From about 450 B.C. onwards the term came to be applied to itinerant teachers (such as Gorgias, Prodicus, Protagoras) who travelled from city to city giving lessons in grammar, rhetoric, politics, mathematics, etc. The sophists, for whom democratic Athens became a haven, were the first to charge a fee for instruction. Their main goal was practical, namely to teach students how to succeed in life and attain material prosperity. To this end they stressed the ability to be persuasive, to argue from any point of view without regard for the truth, attempting to make the weaker argument stronger. At their worst these 'word merchants' encouraged a cynical disbelief in traditional morality, replacing it with the pursuit of selfish ambition; hence the pejorative connotation of the word even today. The chorus of the *Bacchae* considers the wisdom of the sophist folly (395). For other references to sophistry in the play see notes at 201, 270-71, 294, 315, 484.

Sown Men: see 'Cadmus' entry above.

Stage Directions: a) general observations: The stagecraft of fifth-century Greek drama must be inferred from the text; authors did not write stage directions in the modern sense. Fortunately most significant stage action is implicit in the text so that the translator can extrapolate a set of directions for the reader. In one area, however, this issue of staging is problematic. The Greek theater had three points of entry to the acting space: the stage building (*skênê*) and the two side-entrances (*eisodoi*) on the left and right sides of the orchestra. There is no reliable evidence that rigid 'side-entrance' conventions existed in fifth century drama. Each play established its own spatial 'rules.'

b) in the *Bacchae*: It would be convenient if the left side of the stage (from the spectator's perspective) represented the country/mountain and the right side represented the city; convenient because these two offstage areas are the play's dominant geographic poles, symbolic of two opposing worlds (Thebes vs. Mt. Cithaeron, Pentheus vs. Dionysus, culture vs. nature, male vs. female, sanity vs. madness, etc.). I have, in fact, aligned my stage directions to this dichotomy. There is textual evidence, however, that tells against this arrangement. The guards (at 352) as well as Dionysus and Pentheus (at 840, 855, 961) must go *through the city* to reach the mountain. So the road from the palace to Cithaeron passes *through*

Thebes. Hence the scenario *country = stage left, palace = center stage, city = stage right* does not reflect the text's letter. It does, however, reflect the text's spirit which is the main consideration for my general audience. [Cp. Seaford 1996, 148]

Stichomythia: alternating *single* line dialogue. This common convention is used at moments of excitement, controversy, confrontation. There are five examples in the *Bacchae*: 191-99, 463-508, 647-55, 802-44, 1263-1300; variations at 792-801, 923-62 (alternating double lines); 966-70 (alternating half-lines).

Tearing-to-pieces (*sparagmos*): The rending of an animal (goat, fawn, or bull) was one of the three main elements of Dionysiac ritual and the climax of bacchic frenzy; the other two being 'maenads dancing on the mountain' (*oreibasia*) and 'the eating of the animal's raw flesh' (*omophagia*). The rending of Pentheus' cousin Actaeon on Mt. Cithaeron by his own hunting dogs (339), and the tearing up of cattle (735, 739) and of trees (1104) on Cithaeron by the Theban Bacchae are preludes to, and almost caricatures of, the play's horrific climax, the *sparagmos* of Pentheus on Cithaeron by his mother (1127, 1135, 1220).

Thiasos: (plural = *thiasoi*) **a) definition:** a cult group of Dionysiac worshippers whose leader is almost always a woman (sometimes Dionysus himself is the leader). Such is its exclusive use in the *Bacchae* where it appears 13x. Technically *thiasos* refers to "any religious confraternity which existed for the purpose of private as distinct from civic worship; but it describes especially the characteristic unit of organization of Dionysiac religion." [Dodds 70]. Against the usual interpretation that "joining one's soul to the *thiasos*" (line 75) means a merging of individual with group consciousness or the soul's union with god, Leinieks [93] argues that "A *thiasos* is a group of people who have been breathed upon by a god and are under the control of the god. As a result of this divine control the group acts in unison toward a specific goal. The actions themselves are those characteristic of the god. The god's breathing upon and control can be assumed to work on the soul (*psyche*) of each individual in the group... The soul of every member of the thiasos is affected in the same way by the god. The clearest outward expression of the Dionysiac *thiasos* is a *choros* in the sense of a group of dancers." With regard to the impact of 'the god's breath' on the worshipper see 1093n.

b) common traits of *thiasoi*: All share three things: distinctive and identical *appearances* (maenadic garb), *actions* (usually vigorous physical activity such as dancing), and *aims* (worshipping Dionysus). Dionysus, the god of liberation, sees the *thiasos* as an institution of liberation from the violence of Pentheus' palace and city. Hence the place *par excellence* for its activity is the remote wilderness of the mountain (Cithaeron). [Leinieks 319, 338] Historically the *thiasos* is important because it was out of this cult group that the chorus of tragedy and comedy developed. The etymology of the word is unknown; perhaps it is pre-Greek. It is first found in Herodotus (4.79.5).

Thyrsus: (plural = *thyrsi*) a long light fennel-stalk with a bundle of ivy leaves inserted into the stalk's hollow tip (cp. 363, 710). Ivy was the most important element of the thyrsus which was the crucial instrument of Dionysiac worship, serving as a symbol of Bacchus, the god who brings growth to plants, especially the vine. The maenads swung it high in their dance (line 80) and it acted as a sort of sacred magic wand in Dionysiac cult. At first the thyrsus is used for peaceful purposes (e.g. 704-5) but later in the play (762, 1099) more violent uses are found for it (cp. 113n.). Etymologically 'thyrsus' may be related to the Hittite word for 'vine.' [Burkert, 1985, 163; Leinieks 187]. It is first found in Sophocles' *Ichneutai* ('Trackers'), frag. 314. 226R (date unknown but well before the *Bacchae*). Euripides was the first to use the word extensively.

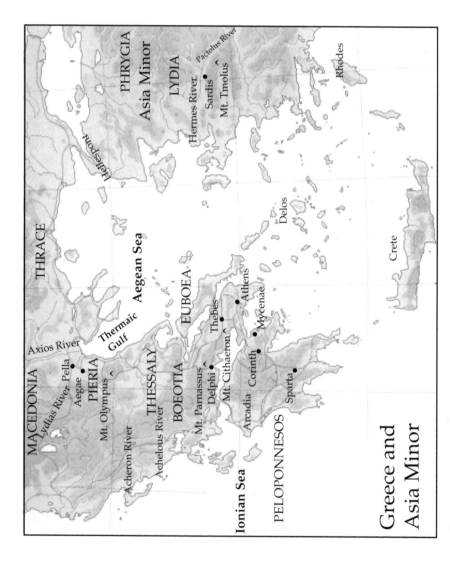

Greece and
Asia Minor

BIBLIOGRAPHY

1. Burkert, W. *Greek Religion* trans. J. Raffan (1985).

2. Burkert, W. *Ancient Mystery Cults* (1987).

3. Carpenter, T. *Dionysian Imagery in Fifth-Century Athens* (1997).

4. Devereux, G. "The Psychotherapy Scene in Euripides' *Bacchae*" *Journal of Hellenic Studies* 90 (1970) 35-48.

5. Dillon, M. "Tragic Laughter" *Classical World* 84 (1991) 345-55.

6. Dodds, E. R. *Euripides: Bacchae*[2] (1960).

7. Dunn, F. *Tragedy's End: Closure and Innovation in Euripidean Drama* (1996).

8. Evans, A. *The God of Ecstasy: Sex Roles and the Madness of Dionysos* (1988).

9. Foley, H. "The Masque of Dionysus" *Transactions of the American Philological Association* 110 (1980) 107-33.

10. Gouldner, A. *Enter Plato: Classical Greece and the Origins of Social Theory* (1965).

11. Henrichs, A. "Greek Maenadism From Olympias to Messalina" *Harvard Studies in Classical Philology* 90 (1978) 121-60.

12. Henrichs, A. "Changing Dionysiac Identities" in *Jewish and Christian Self-Definition* eds. B. Meyer and E. P. Sanders vol. 3 (1982) 137-60, 213-36.

13. Henrichs, A. "Loss of Self, Suffering, Violence: The Modern View of Dionysus from Nietzsche to Girard" *Harvard Studies in Classical Philology* 88 (1984) 205-40.

14. Henrichs, A. "Male Intruders among the Maenads: The So-Called Male Celebrant" in *Mnemai: Classical Studies in Memory of Karl K. Hulley* ed. H. Evjen (1984) 69-92.

15. Kalke, C. "The Making of a Thyrsus: The Transformation of Pentheus in Euripides' *Bacchae*" *American Journal of Philology* 106 (1985) 409-26.

16. Kirk, G. *The Bacchae of Euripides: A Translation with Commentary* (1970).

17. Leinieks, V. *The City of Dionysos: A Study of Euripides' Bakchai* (1996).

18. March, J. "Euripides' *Bacchae*: a Reconsideration in the Light of Vase-Paintings" *Bulletin of the Institute of Classical Studies* 36 (1989) 33-65.

19. Oranje, H. *Euripides' Bacchae: The Play and Its Audience* (1984).

20. Pitt Rivers, J. *Honour and Shame: The Values of Mediterannean Society* ed. J. Peristiany (1966).

21. Rijksbaron, A. *Grammatical Observations on Euripides' Bacchae* (1991).

22. Seaford, R. "Dionysiac Drama and the Dionysiac Mysteries" *Classical Quarterly* 31 (1981) 252-71.

23. Seaford, R. *Reciprocity and Ritual: Homer and Tragedy in the Developing City-State* (1994).

24. Seaford, R. *Euripides' Bacchae with an Introduction, Translation, Commentary* (1996).

25. Segal, C. "Pentheus and Hippolytus on the Couch and on the Grid: Psychoanalytic and Structuralist Readings of Greek Tragedy" in *Interpreting Greek Tragedy* (1986) 268-93.

26. Segal, C. *Dionysiac Poetics and Euripides' Bacchae* (1997; expanded edition whose afterword [pp. 349-93] assesses the most important scholarship on the play since 1982).

27. Segal, C. "Female Mourning and Dionysiac Lament in Euripides' *Bacchae*" in *Orchestra: Drama, Mythos, Bühne* eds. A. Bierl and P. von Möllendorff (1994) 12-18.

28. Seidensticker, B. "Sacrificial Ritual in the *Bacchae*" in *Arktouros: Hellenic Studies Presented to B. M. Knox* ed. M. Putnam et al. (1979) 181-90.

29. Stanford, W. *Ambiguity in Greek Literature* (1939) 174-79.

30. Taplin, O. *Greek Tragedy in Action* (1978).

31. Wolff, C. "Euripides" in *Ancient Writers: Greece and Rome* vol. 1 ed. T. Luce (1982) 233-66.